Roswitha Fischer

Tracing the History of English

Roswitha Fischer

Tracing the History of English

A Textbook for Students

With an Overview of English Literature up to 1790
by Daniela Schwepper

2nd Edition

Cover: schreiberVIS, Seeheim.

Die Deutsche Bibliothek lists this publication
in the Deutsche Nationalbibliografie;
detailed bibliographic data is available in the Internet at
http://dnb.ddb.de.

2nd, unrevised edition 2006
© 2003 by Wissenschaftliche Buchgesellschaft, Darmstadt
Printed on acid-free paper
Printed in Germany

www.wbg-darmstadt.de

ISBN-13: 978-3-534-15135-6
ISBN-10: 3-534-15135-6

CONTENTS

PREFACE

This account of the development of the English language had its origin in an introductory course designed for second and third year students of English philology at the University of Regensburg, Germany. The main task of the course was to familiarize the students with the linguistic history of English, at an introductory level that would then prepare them for more advanced courses to come.

In accordance to this, the text is not intended for the expert, who will quickly realize that there is little fresh material here, but rather for amateurs and students not specializing in other periods of the English language, who are nevertheless examined on historical aspects of English at least at some point in their student life. In this text, they will find a good deal of the available material collected in an easily accessible form; coupled with the various exercises and two comprehensive mock exams (with solutions) which will help them to directly prepare for an exam situation.

The text does not claim to be complete, and its focus on the general may have led to oversimplification in some places, which was accepted due to its practicality and accessibility. The selection of material was made on the basis of the individual preferences of the author on the one hand, and on its usability in class on the other, based upon feedback taken from the students.

Since it is important to put a scientific study in an historic frame, the book starts with an introduction to historical linguistics and the methodology of reconstructing former stages of languages. It then presents a survey of Germanic as long as it is relevant for the later developments of English. The book's main parts deal with Old English, Middle English, and Early Modern English; and it is rounded up by a comparison of British and American English and the situation of English today. The chapters are usually subdivided into parts that give extralinguistic background information and in parts that deal with orthography, phonology, morphology, grammar, and vocabulary of the respective language stage. Each part provides the student with exercises, which are graded according to their degree of difficulty. The detailed solutions to the exercises are given in the appendix. There are also two tests with detailed solutions, as well as an overview of English literature until 1700 written by Daniela Schwepper, and a glossary.

It was decided to write this book in English for several reasons. Firstly, at German universities English is used more and more as the language in which lessons are conducted and exams taken. Secondly, most of the literature referred to was written in English, and last but not least, in English, this book will not only be accessible to German students of English but to any student of the English language.

Roswitha Fischer, Regensburg, 2002

ACKNOWLEDGMENTS

This work, from the way it has grown, owes a lot to earlier scholars, and I will therefore include a general acknowledgment of indebtedness, in particular to the works listed in the bibliography. I am also much obliged to my teachers Ewald Standop, Margret Popp and Wolfgang Obst.

Several of my colleagues have read the work, in manuscript and in proof, and have placed additional material at my disposal. I especially want to thank Florian Schleburg, Daniela Schwepper, Maria Steger and Liselotte Stock for their assistance. Furthermore, I want to thank Ruth Owen and Rachel Harrison for proofreading the English several times and making corrections where necessary. Last but not least, many thanks go to the students in my classes who inspired me and provided me with valuable feedback. Needless to say, the remaining mistakes are on me. I hope that this treatment helps the student grasp the facts easily, deepen the knowledge by means of the applications, and perhaps write a better exam than otherwise possible. If this aim can be reached, the book will have served its purpose.

ABBREVIATIONS AND SYMBOLS

A	Adverbial
acc.	accusative
AmE	American English
BrE	British English
c.	century
dat.	dative
EMidE	Early Middle English
EModE	Early Modern English
gen.	genitive
Gmc	Germanic
GVS	Great Vowel Shift
IE	Indo-European
inf.	informal
IPA	International Phonetic Alphabet
LModE	Late Modern English
MidE	Middle English
neg.	negative
nom.	nominative
O	Object
OE	Old English
OF	Old French
ON	Old Norse
PdE	Present-day English
pl.	plural
pp.	past participle
RP	Received Pronunciation
S	subject
sg.	singular
V	verb
WGmc	West Germanic
✍	easy exercise
✍✍	average exercise
✍✍✍	difficult exercise

TABLE OF EXERCISES

TABLE OF FIGURES

INTRODUCTION

1 Historical Comparative Linguistics

The 19th century witnessed enormous growth and development in the science of language. The studies were historical as well as comparative and focused on the establishment of the Indo-European language family. The concern for regular, common similarities that exist among related languages encouraged the development of reconstruction, and divergent modern forms that were traced back to a single form in the proto-language.

At that time, two scientific paradigms were prevalent: firstly, mechanistic physics, and secondly, the theory of evolution by natural sciences. In mechanistic physics it was claimed that all phenomena could be described by simple, deterministic laws of force and motion. In Charles Darwin's theory of evolution it was maintained that the struggle for existence led to the selection of strong, viable species. Both paradigms had a great impact on the study of language. Sounds were considered to change according to sound laws, and languages were seen as competing with one another in a "struggle for survival". Because of this, scholars started to establish family trees of languages, adopting the techniques used in mapping the evolution of species in biology. Apparently, a language may develop into two or more languages, if any separation of one or more communities takes place and lasts for a considerable length of time. Despite this, it is usually still possible to recognize the common features of the separated languages. It was these similarities that led the historians to assume that the languages of a large part of Europe and part of Asia were at one time identical. The most important discovery leading to this assumption was the recognition that Sanskrit, a language of ancient India, was one of the languages of this group.

Among the outstanding philologists were Rasmus Kristian Rask (1787-1832), Franz Bopp (1791-1867), Jacob Grimm (1785-1863), and August Schleicher (1821-1868). They studied the structure and history of various languages and wrote grammars of them.[1] August Schleicher became widely acknowledged for his *Stammbaum Theory*. He also held the opinion that all languages could be put into the three distinct types of *isolating*, *agglutinating*, and *inflecting* languages.[2] In the last quarter of the century, a group of scholars including Karl Brugmann (1849-1919), August Leskien (1840-1916), Berthold Delbrück (1842-1922), Hermann Osthoff (1847-1909), and Hermann Paul (1846-1921), who wrote *Prinzipien der Sprachgeschichte* in 1880, became known as the *Neogrammarians* (or *Junggrammatiker*). The Neogrammarians wished to make linguistics an exact science, in line with the other natural sciences. Their main hypothesis was the "infallibility of sound laws" which stated that sound change is regular and without exception. Although they were criticized fiercely ("languages are historical creations, not vegetables"), much of the linguistic theory today is based on them.

2 Linguistic Reconstruction

All living languages change, though the rate of change varies from time to time and from language to language. For the modern Icelander, for instance, it is not difficult to read the medieval Icelandic sagas, because changes in the Icelandic language have not been very extreme. But the English find an English document from the year 1300 very troublesome to understand, unless they have some knowledge of Middle English; while an English document from the year 900 (Old English) seems to them to be written in a foreign language.

The changes that have caused the most disagreement are those in pronunciation. There exist various sources of proof for the pronunciation of earlier times, such as the spellings, the treatment of words borrowed from other languages or borrowed by them, the descriptions of contemporary grammarians and spelling reformers, and the modern pronunciation in all the languages and dialects concerned. Several reasons have been brought forward for changes in pronunciation:

a) One reason suggests geographic and climatic factors. It was claimed that people living in a valley were subject to different pronunciation changes from those living in the mountains, but there is no evidence for this.

b) Other researchers have considered biological and racial factors. Once more, no really convincing evidence has been produced; a child of any racial origin that is brought up from birth in an English-speaking family will grow up speaking English just like a native.

c) It is also imaginable that fashion, along with social prestige, plays a part in the process of change. It is certainly involved in the spread of change: one person imitates another, and people with prestige are most likely to be imitated, so that a change in pronunciation that takes place in one social group may be imitated by speakers in another group.

d) Another cause suggested for changes in pronunciation is the fact that the vocal tract of children is still growing. This, however, is unlikely, because humans appear to have a capacity, probably innate, to allow for different sizes of vocal tract when they interpret speech: the voices of a young child, of a woman, and of a deep-voiced man have different pitch levels, but this does not cause problems of comprehension. Furthermore, possible deviations in the language of children are usually corrected in later childhood.

e) What is often involved in sound change is the principle of ease, or the minimization of effort. Since we all try to economize energy in our actions, we also tend to economize the movements of our speech organs, which may initiate a linguistic change. For instance, movements calling for great accuracy or energy may be replaced by less demanding ones. For example, the consonant /m/ in the former Old Norse borrowing *skamt* became an alveolar /n/ under the influence of the following alveolar consonant /t/, cf. Modern English *scant*. This common kind of change is called *assimilation*. Sometimes an existing consonant in a word may even disappear entirely. For example, the /t/ was lost in *castle*, the /w/ in *write*, and the /k/ in *knight*.

2.1 Indo-European

When we look for family relationships between languages, it is helpful to go back to the earliest known forms of the languages. The following table shows the same three words as they appear in Old English, Gothic, Old High German, and Old Norse.[3]

Tab. 1: Comparison of Indo-European Languages

Old English	*stān*	*bān*	*hām*
Gothic	*stains*	–	*haims*
Old High German	*stein*	*bein*	*heim*
Old Norse	*steinn*	*bein*	*heimr*

Because of the similar word forms we can assume a common ancestor, or parent tongue, of the respective languages. This reconstructed ancestor has been called *Proto-Germanic* or simply *Germanic*, which in turn belongs to a far-reaching family of languages, which is usually called *Indo-European*.[4] This family includes most of the languages of Europe and some of India. With its numerous branches and its millions of speakers it has most certainly developed out of some single language, which must have been spoken thousands of years ago by some comparatively small body of people in a relatively restricted geographical area.

It is not certain when, and for how long, the Indo-European people lived together in a single community. Presumably their common life extended over a considerable stretch of time. Their common existence is said to have ended some time between 3500 and 2500 BC but not much is known about their whereabouts. Since the Indo-European languages have a common word for 'winter' and for 'snow', we can conclude that their speakers lived in a cold region; and moreover, words referring to fauna and flora indicate that their original home was in Europe. Archaeological excavations in Russia suggest furthermore that an Indo-European culture existed north of the Caspian sea. At present we maintain that the Indo-Europeans came from an area extending from central Europe to the Ural Mountains.

Fig. 1: The Indo-European Language Tree

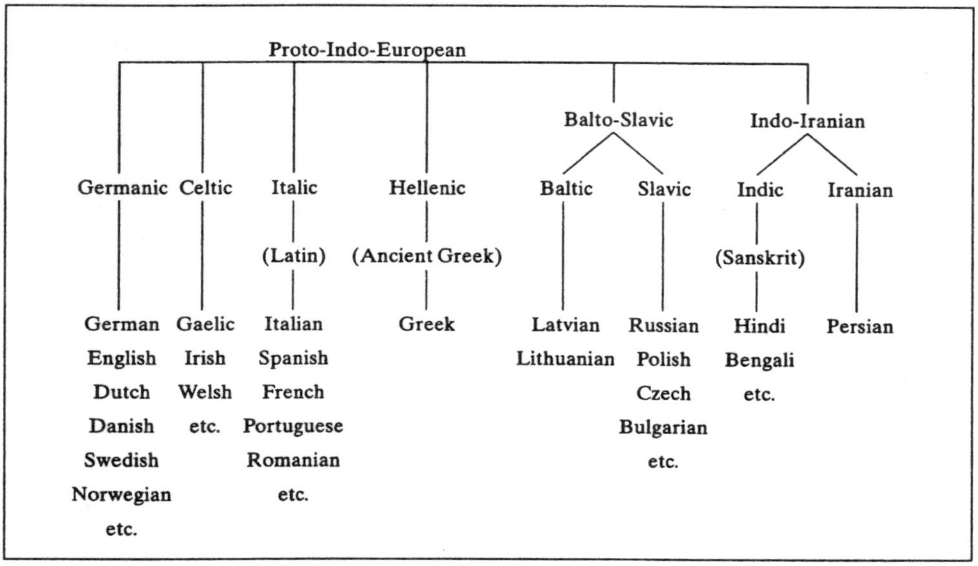

```
                        Proto-Indo-European

                                              Balto-Slavic        Indo-Iranian

  Germanic  Celtic   Italic    Hellenic      Baltic    Slavic    Indic    Iranian

                     (Latin)  (Ancient Greek)                   (Sanskrit)

  German   Gaelic   Italian    Greek        Latvian   Russian   Hindi    Persian
  English  Irish    Spanish                 Lithuanian Polish   Bengali
  Dutch    Welsh    French                            Czech     etc.
  Danish   etc.     Portuguese                        Bulgarian
  Swedish           Romanian                          etc.
  Norwegian         etc.
  etc.
```

The branches of the Indo-European family traditionally fall into two groups according to the transformation that certain consonants of the parent language underwent in each. The groups are based on the development, in very ancient times, of Indo-European palatal $\acute{k}$, and are known as the *centum* and *satem* groups from the words for *hundred* in Latin and Avestan (an ancient Iranian language). The centum

Tab. 2: Words for Numerals in Indo-European, Five of its Daughter Languages, and Hungarian

Indo-European	Sanskrit	Greek	Latin	Gothic	Old Irish	Hungarian
*oykos, *oynos[5]	ékas	heîs	ūnus	ains	oín	egy
*dwō(w)	dvaú	dúō	duo	twai	da	kettő
*treyes	tráyas	treîs	trēs	*þreis	tri	három
*kʷetwores	catváras	téttares	quattuor	fidwor	cethir	négy
*penkʷe	páñca	pénte	quīnque	fimf	cóic	öt
*seks	ṣáṭ	héx	sex	saihs	sé	hat
*septm	saptá	heptá	septem	sibun	secht n-	hét
*oktō(w)	aṣṭaú	oktố	octō	ahtau	ocht n-	nyolc
*newm	náva	ennéa	novem	niun	noí n-	kilenc
*dekm	dáśa	déka	decem	taihun	deich n-	tíz

group includes the Hellenic, Italic, Germanic, and Celtic branches, while Indian, Iranian, Armenian, Balto-Slavic, and Albanian belong to the satem group.

When comparing several Indo-European languages with Hungarian, it is recognizable that Hungarian is not a member of the Indo-European language family. This becomes obvious just by comparing the respective words for the numbers one to ten. For example, the Hungarian words for *four* and *eight* begin with a nasal, while the Indo-European languages have a voiceless plosive or fricative word-initially in *four* and a vowel *a* or *o* in *eight*. The word for *three* in Hungarian is completely different from the corresponding words in the Indo-European languages, and the Hungarian word for *five* does not begin with a consonant but with a vowel. Different syllable structures (consonant–vowel versus vowel–consonant) and different consonantal values at the same position in a word (obstruents versus sonorants) are a clear sign that languages do not belong to the same language family.

🖎 Exercise 1: The Numbers *Four* and *Five* in Various Indo-European Languages[6]

Here are six sets of examples from Indo-European languages, and one from a non-Indo-European language:

	A	B	C	D	E	F	G
'four'	fire	chetyre	cuatro	cztery	yottsu	vier	quattro
'five'	fem	pyat'	cinco	pięć	itsutsu	fünf	cinque

1) Which sample is most likely not to be Indo-European?
2) The remaining six sets can be divided into three pairs of closely related languages. Which examples seem to go together as pairs?
3) With which sets would you associate the English language?
4) With which set would you associate another language which has the cognates *quinque* and *quattuor*?

2.2 Periods of the English Language

The extent to which the English language has changed in the past thousand years can be seen by looking at the different periods and their texts. It is possible to recognize three distinct periods of time (see table 3). Although the dividing lines between the periods are arbitrary, nevertheless certain broad characteristics within each period can be observed. The stage of development from 450-1150 is known as Old English. During that time most of the many inflectional endings were more or less preserved. This changed in the following period of Middle English, which lasted from 1150-1500, by which time inflections had become greatly reduced. Finally we see the advent of Modern English in 1500. By the time we reach this stage in the development, most of the original inflectional systems have disappeared entirely. Modern English includes Present-day English, which covers the time period

Tab. 3: The Periods of the English Language

Old English	450 - 1150
Early	450 - 700
Middle	700 - 900
Standard	900 - 1150
Middle English	1150 - 1500
Early	1100 - 1300
Late	1300 - 1500
Modern English	1500 - 1900
Early	1500 - 1700
Late	1700 - 1900
Present-day English	1900 - today

from 1900 until today. Since 1900 the English language has more or less stayed the same, at least in comparison with former periods.

2.3 Knowledge of Old English

Since Old English speech has not been recorded on tape, and since many texts have been destroyed by fire or other calamities, one may wonder why we still know quite a lot about Early Old English. There are in fact several sources of historical knowledge which enable us to reconstruct the state of the language from that remote period of time. These are:[7]

a) Early glossaries, i.e. lists of Latin words with Old English equivalents, which normally consisted of words that were difficult to understand. The 8th-century *Corpus Glossary*, for instance, has among others the following entries (see table 4). Our knowledge of Latin enables us to translate the Old English words. Moreover, we can recognize a connection between *mis-* and *-byrd* (in *misbyrd*) and modern *mis-* and *birth* respectively, as well as between *bi-* and *-in* (in *binumin*) and German *be-* and *-en* in *benommen*. *Huitfoot* looks a lot like *whitefoot*. We can already suspect that Old English had derivational prefixes and formed adjective + noun compounds of a particular type.

b) Interlinear glosses, i.e. word for word translations of Latin texts. These provided much morphological information (but virtually nothing on syntax, since they follow Latin).

Tab. 4: Comparison between Latin and Old English

Latin	*abortus*	*alnus*	*albipedum*	*ablata*
Old English	*misbyrd*	*aler*	*huitfoot*	*binumin*
Present-day English	*abortion, miscarriage*	*alder*	*white-foot(ed)*	*deprived*

c) Free translations of Latin texts (for instance of the Bible) into idiomatic Old English.

With the help of these sources, we can build up a detailed knowledge of Old English vocabulary, morphology, and syntax. In addition, there also exist several clues to Old English phonology. The spelling ⟨h⟩ will serve as an example. It stood for the old velar fricative /x/ (as in German *Nacht*) at least as late as the 15th century.

d) Our knowledge of typical sound changes. On the whole, arbitrary consonants are not inserted in the middle of words, and loss of segments is more common than gain. (Compare Present-day English /naɪt/ to Old English /nɪxt/).

e) Related languages. Languages related to English show /x/ or a similar fricative, for instance German *Nacht* /naxt/. The only Germanic languages that do not have /x/ here have lost it in all positions (English *night*, Swedish *natt* /natː/ etc.).

f) Regular correspondences of sounds in other Indo-European languages. The phoneme /x/ corresponds to /k/ in Latin *nox* /noks/, stem /nokt-/. Since a fricative is produced with less energy than a stop, Germanic /x/ looks like a weakened survival of an earlier /k/.

g) Treatises on pronunciation from the 16th century onwards. In his *Orthographie*, John Hart describes a consonant in a certain position that he identifies with the letter h, which is clearly [h]. Now if [x] is the natural weakening of [k], [h] is the natural weakening of [x].

h) Modern dialects of English. In the more conservative varieties of modern Scots /x/ is retained, e.g. /nɛxt/ ('night') and /bɔxt/ ('bought').

i) Rhyme. In Middle English, forms in *gh* rhyme only with members of the same class, e.g. *knight*. They do not rhyme with words with the same vowel but no hypothetical /x/, e.g. *delit* (Old French *deliter*).

Thus, by bringing together general linguistic theory, modern dialectology, historical comparative linguistics, and historical evidence, it is possible to create a rather complete description of the earlier stages of English.

Notes:

[1]   E.g. Grimm, Jacob 1819/1837. *Deutsche* [= Germanische] *Grammatik*, 4 vols.

[2]   In isolating languages, each word consists of just one morpheme, as is the case in Vietnamese. In contrast, agglutinating languages "glue" different morphological categories together into one word, as in Turkish. The morphemes indicating morphological categories can be separated from adjacent morphemes. In contrast to this, the segmentation of a grammatical morpheme from other morphemes is difficult in the so-called inflecting languages, as illustrated in Latin.

[3]   Gothic was the language of the Goths, who invaded the Roman Empire, and Old Norse was the early form of the Scandinavian languages.

[4]   Other common names for Indo-European are *Proto-Indo-European* and *Indo-Germanic*.

[5]   An asterisk (*) before a word or a sound-symbol indicates that it is a reconstructed or hypothesized element.

[6]   Based on Yule [2]1996: 223/224.

[7]   Based on Lass 1987: 26-32.

GERMANIC

1 The Branches of Germanic

As a result of the spread of the Germanic-speaking peoples, differences of dialect within Germanic became more marked, and we can now distinguish three main branches or groups of dialects, namely North Germanic, East Germanic, and West Germanic (see figures 2, 3 and 4).

Fig. 2: The North Germanic Languages[1]

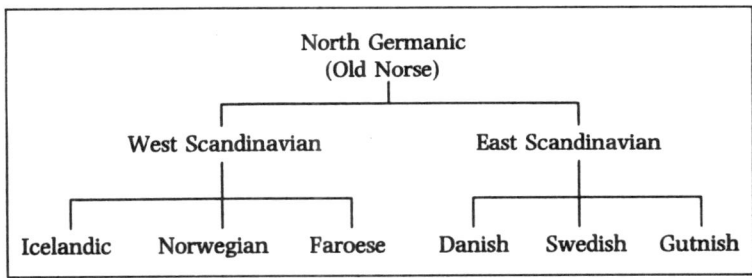

Fig. 3: The East Germanic Languages[2]

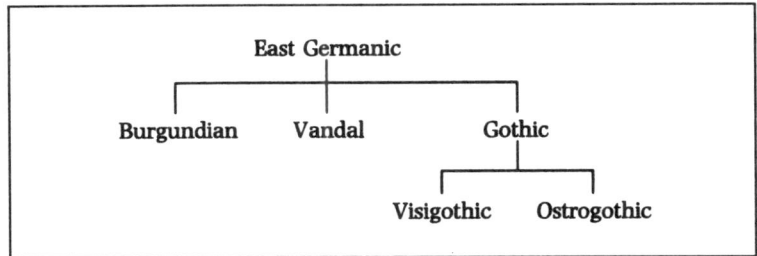

2 From Indo-European to Germanic: Major Changes

Germanic has close ties to the other Indo-European languages together with certain characteristic developments of its own. Like the assumed Indo-European language, Germanic is a highly inflected language. While Indo-European had at least eight cases, Germanic reduced the number of case distinctions to five or six. Moreover, there were various declensions of nouns. All nouns had grammatical gender – every noun was either masculine, feminine, or neuter. Similar concepts apply to adjectives, pronouns, and other words. Indo-European also had a vast array of inflections for its verbs. Germanic kept many of these, but it simplified the system. An alternation of vowels in verbs for grammatical purposes is highly characteristic of the Germanic languages: these verbs are called strong. There are several series of vowels which alternate in this way. Each member of such a series is called a *grade*, and the whole phenomenon is known as *gradation* (or *ablaut*). Examples from Present-day English (an Indo-European inheritance) are *ride – rode – ridden, come – came – come, eat – ate – eaten*, etc. But Germanic also invented a new type, called weak verbs. In these, the past tense is formed by adding a suffix to the verb stem, as in *I talk, I talked*.

Fig. 4: The West Germanic Languages[3]

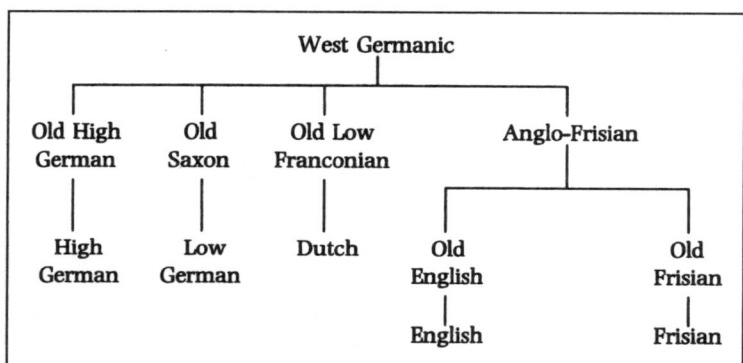

2.1 Grimm's Law

As the *First Sound Shift*, or *Grimm's Law* (after Jacob Grimm, 1822), is such an important distinguishing factor between Germanic and the other Indo-European languages, it will be described here in detail.

Aspirated voiced stops became voiced fricatives and then voiced stops.

Indo-European	>	Proto-Germanic	>	in most Germanic dialects	example		
b^h	>	ƀ	>	b	Latin *frāter*[4]	↔	English *brother*
d^h	>	đ	>	d	Latin *foris*	↔	English *door*
g^h	>	ǥ	>	g	Latin *hostis*	↔	English *guest*

The symbol ƀ represents a voiced labial fricative, đ a voiced interdental fricative, and ǥ a voiced velar fricative.

Voiceless stops became voiceless fricatives. The symbol θ represents a voiceless dental fricative and χ a voiceless palatal or velar fricative; the latter became h word-initially later.

IE	>	Germanic	example	
p	>	f	Latin *pedem*	↔ English *foot*
t	>	θ	Latin *tres*	↔ English *three*
k	>	χ	Latin *cor*	↔ English *heart*

Voiced stops became voiceless stops.

IE	>	Germanic	example	
b	>	p	Russian *jabloko*	↔ English *apple*
d	>	t	Latin *dentis*	↔ English *tooth*
g	>	k	Latin *grānum*	↔ English *corn*

It is likely that these consonant changes took centuries. However, there is an exception to this. It has been called *Verner's Law*, after the Danish scholar Karl Verner, who found an explanation in 1875.

2.2 Verner's Law

Verner's Law states that Germanic voiceless fricatives became voiced when they were in a voiced environment and when the preceding syllable was unstressed. This may have taken place in the first century of our era. After that came the fixing of the accent on the first syllable of the word, which cannot have taken place until after the operation of Verner's Law.

Example: Indo-European t > Germanic θ (Grimm's Law), Germanic θ > ð, as in Indo-European **pət\'er* > Icelandic *faðir* / Old English *fæder*. (The d in *fæder* is a West Germanic development of earlier ð.)

2.3 Other Major Changes

a) A free accentual system developed in Germanic into a fixed one: we regularly find stressed first syllables. Exceptions like the modern English word *believe* /bɪ'li:v/ occur when the initial syllable was a prefix.

b) The Indo-European o changed into a (e.g. Latin *octō*, Gothic *ahtau*), and Indo-European $\bar{a}$ became $\bar{o}$ (e.g. Latin *māter*, Old English *mōdor*).

c) All Indo-European distinctions of tense and aspect were lost in the verb except for the present and past tenses. This simplification is reflected in all the languages that have developed out of Germanic (e.g. English *bind – bound*, German *binden – band*).

d) Germanic has a large number of words that are not known in any other Indo-European language. It is assumed that these words are distinctively Germanic. The vocabulary is mainly restricted to seafaring terms, e.g. *ship, sail, boat, sea*, etc. There are also words of everyday use, such as *broad, drink, drive, meat, rain, wife*.

e) Moreover, Germanic developed a preterite tense form with a 'dental suffix' (i.e. one containing a *t* or *d*). This led to all Germanic languages having two types of verbs. The weak verbs, on the one hand, employ the dental suffix (*walk – walked*), the strong verbs, on the other hand, show an internal vowel change (*rise – rose*). Many of the originally strong verbs have become weak nowadays.

f) Although English has lost all declensions of the adjective, the older forms of Germanic had two ways of declining adjectives. The weak declension was used mainly when the adjective modified a noun and was preceded by an article (cf. German *die jungen Frauen*), otherwise the strong declension was used (cf. German *junge Frauen*).

✍ ✍ ✍ Exercise 2: Major Changes from Indo-European to Germanic[5]

Consider the following Germanic features:

A a fixed stress on the first syllable
B certain vowel changes ($o > a$, $\bar{a} > \bar{o}$)
C Grimm's Law (including Verner's Law)
D a dental suffix for the preterite tense
E "strong" versus "weak" adjectives

Forms from a non-Germanic but Indo-European language are listed together with the parallel form from a Germanic language. Compare the forms with one another, then identify the Germanic characteristic that each example clearly illustrates.

1) Latin		Old English	
magnus homō	'a great man'	*micel guma*	'a great man'
iste magnus homō	'that great man'	*se micla guma*	'that great man'
magnī hominēs	'great men'	*micle guman*	'great men'
istī magnī hominēs	'those great men'	*þā miclan guman*	'those great men'
2) Latin		Old English	
edō	'eat'	*etan*	'eat'
augeō	'increase'	*īecan*	'eke'

3) Sanskrit		Old English	
bhrūs	'brow'	*brū*	'brow'
rudhiras	'red'	*rēad*	'red'
janghā	'heel, lower leg'	*gangan*	'go'(cf. *gangway*)
4) Greek 'mother'		Old English 'mother'	
mḗter	(nom. sg.)	*mōdor*	(nom. sg.)
mētrós	(gen. sg.)	*mōdor*	(gen. sg.)
mētrí	(dat. sg.)	*mēder*	(dat. sg.)
mētéres	(nom. pl.)	*mōdor*	(nom. pl.)
mētérōn	(gen. pl.)	*mōdra*	(gen. pl.)
mētrási	(dat. pl.)	*mōdrum*	(dat. pl.)
5) Latin		Old English	
frāter	'brother'	*brōðor*	'brother'
fāgus	'beech tree'	*bōc*	'beech tree'
māter	'mother'	*mōdor*	'mother'
6) Latin		Old English	
sāgiō	'I scent'	*ic sēce*	'I seek'
sāgīvī	'I scented'	*ic sōhte*	'I sought'
domō	'I tame'	*ic temme*	'I tame'
domuī	'I tamed'	*ic temede*	'I tamed'

Notes:

[1] Taken from Barber 1993: 84.

[2] Taken from Barber 1993: 85.

[3] Taken from Barber 1993: 86.

[4] In Latin, the Indo-European b^h and d^h developed into *f*, and the Indo-Eurpean g^h changed to *h*.

[5] Slightly adapted from Algeo [4]1993: 107.

OLD ENGLISH

1 Historical Background

The Old English period can be divided into smaller units: Early Old English (before 700), Middle Old English (700-900), and Standard Old English (900-1150). There is very little documentation of Old English before 700. Literacy was introduced only after the arrival of the Roman missionaries. Monastic centers grew rapidly, and a large number of Latin manuscripts were produced. This increasingly literate climate led writers to begin writing texts in Old English. However, the material remaining from the Old English period is extremely small. Most of the extant Old English manuscripts are from the period following the reign of King Alfred (849-899). Since they were written down or copied in Late West Saxon, there is little evidence of the other Old English dialects.

1.1 Desirable Britain

Around the middle of the first millenium BC Celtic tribes settled in the British Isles. There were two main Celtic groups: the *Goidelic* or *Gaelic Celts* and the *Cymric* or *Britannic Celts*. The languages of the Gaelic Celts, namely *Irish Gaelic* and *Scottish Gaelic*, have survived until today; *Welsh* and *Breton* are the modern representatives of the languages of the Britannic Celts.

Tab. 5: The History of the Settlements in the British Isles Beginning with the Celts

600 or 500 BC	The Celts arrived in Britain.
55/54 BC	Julius Caesar made attempts to invade Britain but failed.
43 AD	Roman Emperor Claudius conquered Britain.
410	The Roman occupation ended.
449	The Angles, Saxons, Jutes, and Frisians conquered Britain.
597	Roman Christian missionaries began to christianize Britain.
789	The Scandinavians began to attack Britain.
9th century	North-East England was ruled by Scandinavians (886 Danelaw).
1016-1035 (1035-1042)	The whole of England was governed by the Danish King Cnut (and his sons).
1042	Edward, the Confessor, regained the throne.

In 55 BC Julius Caesar invaded England but he soon returned to Gaul. Almost a century later, Emperor Claudius undertook the actual conquest of the island and made it part of the Roman Empire for about 400 years. After the Roman legionnaires were withdrawn in the early fifth century, Picts from the north and Scots from the West attacked the now unprotected British Celts, who ironically enough asked Germanic tribes for assistance. According to the Venerable Bede's report of the invasion of Britain in his *Ecclesiastical History of the English People*, written in Latin and completed in 730, ships of Germanic warriors began to arrive in 449.

The home land of the Old Saxons was in North-West Germany (in Schleswig-Holstein, and perhaps farther west, too, along the North Sea coast). The Angles probably came from slightly farther north, from the Danish mainland and islands. The origin of the Jutes is less clear – they may have come from Jutland, but their culture seems to have had bonds with that of the Franks further south, and some people believe that they came from the Rhineland. There is also evidence that in addition to Angles, Saxons, and Jutes, the Germanic invaders included Frisians.

Fig. 5: The Origins of the Germanic Tribes[1]

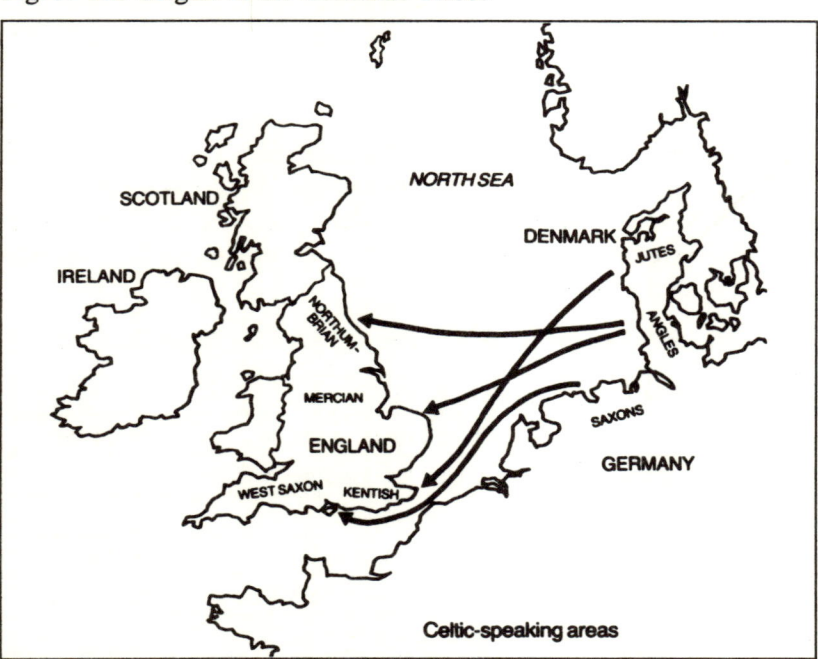

In the following period, the two main influences of the Anglo-Saxon rule and culture were firstly Christianization and secondly Scandinavian invasions. The Scandinavians even became the rulers of England in the eleventh century. It is imaginable that the Scandinavian settlers assimilated well into the Anglo-Saxon culture, and due to the similarities of their languages, the English language still remained English.

1.2 The Anglo-Saxon Heptarchy

The Germanic settlement grew into the so-called *Anglo-Saxon heptarchy* – that is, the country of seven kingdoms: Northumbria, Mercia, East Anglia, Essex, Kent, Sussex, and Wessex.

Fig. 6: The Anglo-Saxon Heptarchy[2]

The grouping, however, was not very permanent. Sometimes two kingdoms were united under one king, or kingdoms were divided under separate rulers. In the seventh century Northumbria became the chief center of culture and wealth; in the eighth century its supremacy was passed to Mercia and finally, in the ninth century, to Wessex. In the following period of time the West Saxon kings were able to maintain the claim to be kings of all the English.

1.3 The Old English Dialects

Since the English people originally came from various parts of Western Europe, they spoke different dialects of West Germanic. Kentish was the language of the Jutes who settled in Kent and the Isle of Wight. West Saxon was spoken in the region south of the Thames with the exception of Kent. Mercian was heard from the Thames to the Humber except for Wales; and Northumbrian was the dialect spoken north of the Humber.[3]

The unification of England under the West Saxon kings in the ninth century led to the gradual development of the late West Saxon dialect as a literary standard.

Fig. 7: The Old English Dialects[4]

1.4 The Name of the Language

The Germanic tribes called the Celts 'foreigners' (*wēalas*), who in turn called the invaders 'Saxons', regardless of their tribe. By the end of the sixth century, however, the term 'Saxons' had been replaced by 'Angles' (Latin *Anglī*). The word is derived from the name of the Angles (Old English *Engle*), but was used for any Germanic inhabitant of the island. Likewise, the land and its people were called 'Angle-kin' or 'people of the Angles' (*Angelcynn*) early on. From about the year 1000, *Englaland* ('land of the Angles') from which came *England*, began to take its place. The corresponding adjective was *Englisc*, which from the very beginning had been used by writers for the English language. The name for the language is thus older than the name for its speakers.

2 Spelling and Pronunciation

2.1 The Alphabet

Old English was first written using runes, which were devised for carving on wood or stone by the Germanic peoples of Scandinavia, present-day Germany and the British Isles. These runes were initially associated with pagan mysteries – the word *rune* means 'secret'. The runic alphabet is called *futhorc*, from the names of its first letters. It consisted of 24 letters, which could be read right to left and left to right, and used newly introduced letters to cope with the range of Old English sounds.[5]

Fig. 8: The First Letters of the Runic Alphabet

feoh	ūr	þorn	ōs	rād	cēn
f	u	þ	o	r	c

The use of runes does not seem to have been widespread. Only after the Christianization of England did writing become more general. The script used by the clerics is called *insular hand*, which was an Irish version of the Roman alphabet. It had rounded letters, each distinct and easy to recognize. The following letters are different from Present-day English:

⟨æ⟩ called *ash*, derived from Latin, representing a vowel pronounced /æ/, /æː/,

⟨ð⟩ called *eth*, derived from Irish writing (a modification of Latin ⟨d⟩), representing a consonant pronounced /θ/ or /ð/,

⟨þ⟩ called *thorn* from its runic name (borrowed from the futhorc), representing a consonant pronounced /θ/or /ð/,

⟨p⟩ called *wynn*, borrowed from the futhorc, representing a consonant pronounced /w/, replacing ⟨u⟩ or ⟨uu⟩ used in earlier Old English writing,

⟨ȝ⟩ called *yogh*, an Irish modification of Latin ⟨g⟩, which could be pronounced [g], [j], or [ɣ], depending on the neighboring sounds.

Several of the Roman letters, notably ⟨f⟩, ⟨g⟩, ⟨r⟩, ⟨s⟩, and ⟨t⟩, had distinctive shapes. There were even three shapes for ⟨s⟩: ⟨s⟩, ⟨ſ⟩ and ⟨ſ⟩.

✍ Exercise 3: Insular Hand I

Aelfric (circa 955-1010) was the Abbot of Eynshām near Oxford and a famous English preacher and grammarian. Below you find the beginning of one of his sermons, which is written in the insular hand.[6]

Ælfric abb. gret Sigeferþ freondlice; Me is gesæd þ ðu sædest beo me þ ic oþer tæhte on Engliscen gewriten. oþer eower ancor æt ham mid eow tæhþ. forþan ðe he swutelice sægþ þ hit sie alefd. þ mæsse preostas wel motan wifigen. and min gewriten wiþcweþeþ ðysen.	Aelfric abbot greets Sigeferth friendlily; me is said that thou said'st by me that I other taught in English writings, other your anchorite[7] at home with you teacheth, for he clearly saith that it be permitted that mass priests well may wive, and my writings gainsay this.

Rewrite the given word for word translation in contemporary English.

✍✍ Exercise 4: Insular Hand II

King Alfred (849-901) ordered the recording of important events of English history, known as the *Anglo-Saxon Chronicle* which has survived in several manuscripts, with the *Peterborough Chronicle* being one of them. The excerpt below is the opening of the *Peterborough Chronicle*.[8]

Brittene igland is ehta hund mila lang ⁊ twa hund brad. ⁊ her sind on þis iglande fif geþeode. englisc. ⁊ brittisc. ⁊ wilsc. ⁊ scyttisc. pyhtisc. ⁊ boc leden. Erest weron bugend þises landes brittes.	Brittene igland is ehta hund mila lang ⁊ twa hund brad. ⁊ her sind on þis iglande fif geþeode. englisc. ⁊ brittisc. ⁊ wilsc. ⁊ scyttisc. pyhtisc. ⁊ boc leden. Erest weron bugend þises landes brittes.

1) Give a word for word translation of this text. These words will assist you: *geþeode* 'languages', *boc leden* 'book Latin', *bugend* 'inhabitants'.
2) After you have read 2.2, give a phonetic transcription of the text.
3) Give a free translation of the text.

2.2 Old English Pronunciation

Our knowledge of Old English can only be approximate. Pronunciation and spelling were much closer in Old English than today. As a rule each letter was pronounced as one sound. Sometimes one letter could represent different sounds.

The vowel letters in Old English were ⟨a⟩, ⟨æ⟩, ⟨e⟩, ⟨i⟩, ⟨o⟩, ⟨u⟩, and ⟨y⟩. They represented both short and long vowels.[9] There were two diphthong letters: ⟨ea⟩, which stood for [æɑ] (and [æᵒ]), and ⟨eo⟩, which represented [eo] most of the time. In Late Old English, these diphthongs became monophthongs, some of which were ultimately fused into the same monophthong [iː], as in *beat* from Old English *bēatan* and *creep* from Old English *crēopan*.

Tab. 6: The Old English Vowels

Old English vowels	phonetic symbols (IPA)	Old English examples	Present-day English examples (RP)
⟨i⟩	[ɪ]	*findan* 'find'	*sit*
	[iː]	*fīf* 'five'	*see*
⟨y⟩	[ʏ]	*cyning* 'king'	German *Mücke*
	[yː]	*hȳran* 'hear'	German *grün*
⟨e⟩	[ɛ]	*helm* 'helm'	*helmet*
	[eː]	*mētan* 'meet'	German *legen*
⟨æ⟩	[æ]	*dæg* 'day'	*hat*
	[æː]	*dǣd* 'deed'	German *zäh*
⟨a⟩	[ɑ]	*habban* 'have'	German *Hast*
	[ɑː]	*hām* 'home'	*calm*
⟨o⟩	[ɔ]	*sorh* 'sorrow'	*hot*
	[oː]	*lōcian* 'look'	German *Bohne*
⟨u⟩	[ʊ]	*sum* 'some'	*put*
	[uː]	*mūþ* 'mouth'	*moon*
⟨ea⟩	[æᵒ]	*eald* 'old'	(no equivalents)
	[æɑ]	*ēast* 'east'	
⟨eo⟩	[ɛᵓ]	*heofon* 'heaven'	(no equivalents)
	[eo]	*prēost* 'priest'	

The consonant letters in English could be pronounced both short and long. Their length was indicated by the doubling of consonant symbols, as in *cunnan* ('know') or *sittan* ('sit'). Both of the doubled consonants were to be pronounced, for instance *habban* ['hɑbːɑn]. See table 7 below.

The pronunciation of some of the letters depended on their phonological environment. Thus the letters ⟨s⟩ or ⟨ſ⟩, ⟨þ⟩ or ⟨ð⟩, and ⟨f⟩ were regularly pronounced voiced between voiced sounds, but voiceless word-initially, word-finally, and when doubled.

The pronunciation of ⟨g⟩, ⟨c⟩ and ⟨h⟩ depended largely on whether the neighboring vowels were front or back vowels, at least in Early Old English. Thus ⟨h⟩ stood for the velar fricative [x] after back vowels and for the palatal fricative [ç] after front vowels. In the initial position, it was pronounced [h]. If ⟨c⟩ was next to a back vowel, it indicated the velar stop [k]; if it was next to a front vowel, the sound was pronounced as the affricate [tʃ]. Preconsonantal ⟨c⟩ was always [k].

Tab. 7: The Old English Consonants[10]

Old English consonants	phonetic symbols (IPA)	Old English examples	Present-day English equivalents (RP)
⟨p⟩	[p]	*pund* 'pound'	*p*ound
⟨b⟩	[b]	*bēon* 'be'	*b*e
⟨t⟩	[t]	*tō* 'to'	*t*o
⟨d⟩	[d]	*draca* 'ragon'	*d*ragon
⟨c⟩	[k] [tʃ]	*clǣne* 'clean' *cirice* 'church'	*c*lean *ch*urch
⟨g⟩ (⟨ȝ⟩)	[g] [j] [ɣ]	*gān* 'go' *gēar* 'year' *fugol* 'bird'	*g*o *y*ear dialectal *Vogel*[11]
⟨cg⟩ (⟨cȝ⟩)	[dʒ]	*brycg* 'bridge'	bri*dg*e
⟨x⟩	[ks]	*æx* 'axe'	a*x*e
⟨f⟩	[f] [v]	*fōt* 'foot' *ofer* 'over'	*f*oot o*v*er
⟨þ⟩ or ⟨ð⟩	[θ] [ð]	*þing* 'thing' *ōþer* 'other'	*th*ing o*th*er
⟨s⟩ or ⟨ſ⟩	[s] [z]	*sellan* 'sell' *cēosan* 'choose'	*s*ell choo*s*e
⟨sc⟩	[ʃ] [sk]	*scip* 'ship' *āscian* 'ask'	*sh*ip a*sk*
⟨h⟩	[h] [ç] [x]	*hand* 'hand' *wiht* 'creature' *þōhte* 'thought'	*h*and German *Wicht* German *dachte*
⟨l⟩	[l]	*land* 'land'	*l*and
⟨m⟩	[m]	*mīn* 'mine'	*m*ine
⟨n⟩	[n]	*niht* 'night'	*n*ight
⟨r⟩	[r]	*rīce* 'kingdom'	*r*ealm
⟨w⟩ (⟨ƿ⟩)	[w]	*wīf* 'woman'	*w*oman

The letter ⟨g⟩ stood for the voiced velar stop [g] before consonants and word-initially before back vowels. It stood for a voiced velar fricative [ɣ] in the neighborhood of back vowels. In most of the positions, i.e. in the neighborhood of front vowels, the symbol indicated [j]. The digraphs ⟨cg⟩ and ⟨sc⟩ (later ⟨sh⟩) were usually pronounced [dʒ] (or [d:ʒ]) and [ʃ] respectively. See the following table.

Tab. 8: Rules for the Consonantal Allophones of Old English

letter	sound(s)	position
⟨f⟩	[f]	word-initially / word-finally (*hlāf* [hlɑːf], 'loaf')
	[v]	between voiced sounds (*drīfan* ['driːvan], 'to drive')
⟨s⟩	[s]	word-initially / word-finally / when doubled (*sunu* ['sʊnʊ], 'son')
	[z]	between voiced sounds (*lēosan* ['leozan], 'to lose')
⟨ð, þ⟩	[θ]	word-initially / word-finally (*þorn* [θɔrn], 'thorn')
	[ð]	between voiced sounds (*brōðor* ['broːðɔr] 'brother')
⟨c⟩	[k]	pre-consonantal and next to back vowels (at least in Early Old English; *cnāwan* ['knɑːwan], 'to know')
	[tʃ]	next to front vowels (*cild* [tʃɪld], 'child'; *ic* [ɪtʃ], 'I')
⟨g⟩	[j]	next to front vowels (*gēar* [jæɑr], 'year')
	[g]	before consonants and before back vowels (*glæd* [glæd], 'glad')
	[ɣ]	between and after back vowels: as a voiced velar fricative (*dagas* ['dɑɣɑs], 'days')
⟨h⟩	[h]	word-initially (*habban* ['habːan], 'to have')
	[ç]	after a front vowel (like German *ich*; *miht* [mɪçt], 'might')
	[x]	after a back vowel (like German *ach*; *seah* [sæᵃx], 'saw')

✍✍ Exercise 5: Phonetic Transcription

Write these words in phonetic transcription:

1) *fyxen*   'vixen'
2) *wīf*   'woman'
3) *wīfes*   'woman's'
4) *bæð*   'bath'
5) *baðian*   'to bathe'
6) *sǣs*   'seas'
7) *nosu*   'nose'
8) *lȳs*   'lice'
9) *lūsa*   'of lice'
10) *hām*   'home'
11) *hring*   'ring'

12) *hlynsian*   'to resound'
13) *āhte*   'owned'
14) *eoh*   'horse'
15) *scēap*   'sheep'
16) *sceaft*   'shaft'
17) *brycg*   'bridge'
18) *dæges*   'day's'

Reminder: Back and Front Vowels

In the chart (a vowel trapezoid) that follows, the vowels of Present-day English are shown according to the position of the tongue relative to the roof of the mouth (high, mid, low) and to the position of the highest part of the tongue (front, central, back).

Fig. 9: The Vowel Trapezoid (RP)[12]

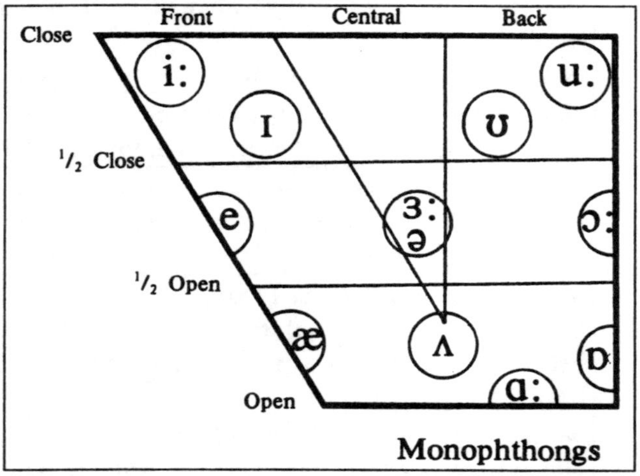

✍ Exercise 6: The Letters ⟨c⟩ and ⟨g⟩

Examine the following words. Each group of words illustrates a typical position for the letters ⟨c⟩ and ⟨g⟩. If the prehistoric form of the word is relevant, it is given as a reconstruction with the usual *asterisk.

A ⟨c⟩ in *clif* 'cliff', *cniht* 'boy', *āc* 'oak', *munuc* 'monk'
B ⟨c⟩ in *ceorl* 'churl', *cīdan* 'to chide', *micel* 'much', *bēce* 'beech'
C ⟨c⟩ in *pic* 'pitch', *līc* 'body', *brēc* 'breeches', *swelc* 'such' (*swalīc)
D ⟨c⟩ in *catt* 'cat', *cōl* 'cool', *nacod* 'naked', *sūcan* 'to suck'
E ⟨g⟩ in *gāt* 'goat', *guma* 'man', *gylden* 'golden' (*guldīn), *gæt* 'goats' (*gātiz)
F ⟨g⟩ in *glæs* 'glass', *grimm* 'fierce', *gnorn* 'sad', *gleomu* 'splendor'
G ⟨g⟩ in *īg* 'island', *sægde* 'said', *sige* 'victory', *þegnas* 'thanes'
H ⟨g⟩ in *sagu* 'saying', *swōgan* 'to sound', *āgan* 'to own', *bōg* 'bough', *boga* 'bow'
I ⟨g⟩ in *geard* 'yard', *gē* 'ye', *geolu* 'yellow', *gimm* 'gem'

1) For each group of words, decide whether ⟨c⟩ represents [k] or [tʃ] and whether ⟨g⟩ represents [g] or [ɣ] or [j].
2) Which sounds occur before consonants or before back vowels (or front vowels resulting from mutation)?
3) Which sounds occur after or between back vowels?
4) Which sounds occur next to front vowels?

✍ ✍ Exercise 7: Bede's *Ecclesiastical History*

This document describes the beginning of the coming of the missionaries to England under Saint Augustine in 597.[13] Read the text aloud. Then transcribe the italicized words in the original version.

Ðā wæs on þā tīd Æþelbeorth *cyning* hāten on *Centrīce*, and *mihtig*: hē *hæfde* rīce oð *gemǣru* Humbre strēames, sē tōscādeþ sūðfolc Angelþēode and norðfolc. Ðonne is on ēasteweardre Cent *micel* ēaland, Tenet, þæt is siex hund hīda micel æfter Angelcynnes *eahte*... On *þyssum* ēalande cōm ūp sē Godes þēow Augustinus and his gefēran; wæs hē fēowertiga sum. Nāmon hīe ēac swelce him wealhstōdas of Franclande mid, swā him Sanctus Gregorius bebēad. And þā sende tō Æþelbeorthe ǣrendwrecan and onbēad þæt hē of Rōme cōme and þæt betste ǣrende *lǣdde*; and sē þe him hīersum bēon wolde, būton twēon hē gehēt ēcne gefēan on heofonum and tōweard rīce būton ende mid þone sōþan God and þone lifigendan. [...] Ðā wæs æfter manigum *dagum* þæt sē cyning cōm tō þǣm ēalande, and hēt him ūte setl *gewyrcean*; and hēt Augustinum mid his gefērum þider tō his *sprǣce* cuman. Warnode hē him þȳ lǣs hīe on *hwelc* hūs tō him inēoden; brēac ealdre hēalsunga, gif hīe hwelcne drȳcræft hæfden þæt hīe hine oferswīðan and beswīcan sceolden...

Then (there) was at that time a king named Æthelberht in Kent, and (a) mighty (one): he had dominion up to (the) confines of the Humber river, which separates the south folk of the English and the north folk. There is in eastward Kent a large island, Thanet, that is six hundred hides large after the reckoning of the English... On this island came up the servant of God, Augustine, and his companions; he was one of forty. Took they likewise with them interpreters from Frankland, as them Saint Gregory bade. And then (Augustine) sent to Æthelberht a messenger and announced that he from Rome had come and the best message brought (led); and he who (if any) would be obedient to him, without doubt he promised eternal happiness in heaven and a future kingdom without end with the true God and the living (God). Then it was after many days that the king came to the island and commanded (them) in the open air a seat to make him; and he bade Augustine with his companions to come thither to a (his) consultation. He guarded himself lest they in any house with him should enter: he employed an old precaution in case they any sorcery had with which they should overcome and get the better of him...

---

3 Major Sound Changes in Old English

In prehistoric Old English, a number of combinative sound changes took place. Certain vowels were fronted, raised or even diphthongized through the influence of neighboring sounds. The exact dates of these various sound changes are unknown, but they must have taken place sometime between the fourth and the eighth centuries. The following changes are treated in the probable order of their occurrence.[14]

3.1 First Fronting

Except before nasals and before back vowels in the following syllable, low back [ɑ] was raised to [æ]. By this process, the new short vowel [æ] emerged.

Example: Gothic *dags* – Old English *dæg* (but Old English plural nominative and accusative: *dagas*)

3.2 Breaking

Breaking is the diphthongization of front vowels in certain sound environments: a) before /r/ + consonant or /l/ + consonant, and b) before the velar fricative /x/. Thus the vowel [ɛ] was for instance diphthongized to [ɛ°], and the vowel [æ] to [æ°].

Examples: **werpan > weorpan* ('to throw', German *werfen*)
            *wærp > wearp ('(she) threw' – strong verb of class III)
            *hælp > healp ('(she) helped')
            *fehu > feoh ('cattle', German *Vieh*)

3.3 I-Mutation (I-Umlaut or Front Mutation)

I-mutation is the fronting or raising of a vowel by partial assimilation to an [ɪ], [iː] or a [j] sound in the following syllable. When in Early Old English *i* or *j* followed a stressed syllable, low front vowels were raised and back vowels were fronted. The front vowel [æ] changed to [ɛ], and [ɛ] changed to [ɪ]; the back vowels [ʊ] and [uː] became [ʏ] and [yː]; [ɔ] and [oː] became [œ] and [øː] respectively, later [ɛ] and [eː]; and [ɑ] and [ɑː] changed into [æ] and [æː]. All the diphthongs became [ɪʸ] and [iy] respectively, later [ɪ], [iː] or [ʏ], [yː]. Subsequently, the [ɪ], [iː] and [j], which had caused the mutation, disappeared or changed to [ɛ], later [ə].

The principle of i-mutation explains the relationship between a number of Old English (and Present-day English) words which may otherwise not be apparent. The following categories in particular were affected:

a) irregular plurals, for example *mūs / mȳs* ('mouse' / 'mice'), *fōt / fēt* ('foot' / 'feet'), *man / men* ('man' / 'men')

b) deadjectival, feminine abstract nouns, for example *hāl / hælþ* ('whole' / 'health'), *strang / strengþ* ('strong' / 'strength')

c) comparative, superlative forms of adjectives, for example *eald* / *ieldra* / *ieldest* ('old' / 'elder' / 'eldest')

d) denominal adjectives, for example *gold* (Germanic *gulþa* 'gold') / *gylden* ('golden')

e) 2nd and 3rd person singular indicative of strong verbs, for example *helpan* / *þu hilpst* / *he hilpþ* ('to help' / 'you help' / 'he helps')

f) class I of the weak verbs derived by adding *-jan*
   – from nouns, e.g. *talu* ('tale') + *-jan* > *tellan* ('to tell')
   – from adjectives, e.g. *full* ('full') + *-jan* > *fyllan* ('to fill')
   – from strong verbs, marking causation, e.g. *sat-* (stem form of *sittan* 'to sit') + *-jan* > *settan* ('to set')

3.4 Velar Umlaut (Back-Mutation, Back Umlaut)

The velar umlaut can also be considered a kind of breaking before back vowels. Compared to the breaking of front vowels, it is much more sporadic and affects only short vowels. It occurs more regularly in Mercian and Kentish than in West Saxon. Before back vowels in the following syllable, the short front vowels [ɪ], [ɛ] and [æ] attained a vowel glide and now occurred as ⟨io⟩ and ⟨ea⟩.

Examples: *ælu* > *ealu* ('ale')
          hefon > *heofon* ('heaven')
          witan > *wiotan* ('to know')

🖎🖎 Exercise 8: Mutated Vowels[15]

In the following examples, the first word in each pair has an unmutated vowel, and the second word in each pair is a related form with a mutated vowel omitted from its spelling. Supply the missing letter.

1)	*bacan*	'bake'	-	*b_cþ*	'(she) bakes'
2)	*sægde*	'said'	-	*s_cgan*	'to say'
3)	*helpan*	'to help'	-	*h_lpþ*	'(she) helps'
4)	*gāt*	'goat'	-	*g_t*	'goats'
5)	*fōda*	'food'	-	*f_dan*	'feed'
6)	*full*	'full'	-	*f_llan*	'to fill'
7)	*mā*	'more'	-	*m_st*	'most'
8)	*fūl*	'foul'	-	*f_lþ*	'filth'
9)	*hēah*	'high'	-	*h_ra*	'higher'

4 Grammar

4.1 Nouns, Pronouns and Adjectives[16]

Old English distinguishes number, case, and gender, in nouns, pronouns, and adjectives. The numbers are singular and plural, a dual being found in the 1st and 2nd personal pronouns. The main cases are nominative, accusative, genitive, and dative. In addition, in certain parts of the adjective and pronoun declension an instrumental occurs. There are three genders: masculine, feminine, and neuter.

Old English nouns are traditionally divided into weak and strong nouns. A common Old English declension was that of *a*-stems (*a* was the sound with which their stems ended in Proto-Germanic). It was in time to be extended to practically all nouns.

Tab. 9: Old English Noun Declensions

	masculine *a*-stem	neuter *a*-stem	*r*-stem	*n*-stem[17]	root-consonant-stem	*ō*-stem
	'dog'	'animal'	'child'	'ox'	'foot'	'gift'
nom. sg.	*hund*	*dēor*	*cild*	*oxa*	*fōt*	*giefu*
gen. sg.	*hundes*	*dēores*	*cildes*	*oxan*	*fōtes*	*giefe*
dat. sg.	*hunde*	*dēore*	*cilde*	*oxan*	*fēt*	*giefe*
acc. sg.	*hund*	*dēor*	*cild*	*oxan*	*fōt*	*giefe*
nom. pl.	*hundas*	*dēor*	*cildru*	*oxan*	*fēt*	*giefa*
gen. pl.	*hunda*	*dēora*	*cildra*	*oxna*	*fōta*	*giefa*
dat. pl.	*hundum*	*dēorum*	*cildrum*	*oxum*	*fōtum*	*giefum*
acc. pl.	*hundas*	*dēor*	*cildru*	*oxan*	*fēt*	*giefa*

There were two demonstratives in Old English. The more common one, which is illustrated below, developed into the modern definite article *the*. The form of the demonstrative is the main clue to the gender of the noun.

Tab. 10: Old English Demonstratives

	masculine	neuter	feminine	plural
nominative	*sē, se*	*þæt*	*sēo*	*þā*
genitive	*þæs*	*þæs*	*þǣre*	*þāra*
dative	*þǣm*	*þǣm*	*þǣre*	*þǣm*
accusative	*þone*	*þæt*	*þā*	*þā*
instrumental	*þȳ, þon, þē*	*þȳ, þon, þē*	–	–

Most adjectives can be declined strong or weak. The strong form is used when the adjective stands alone, or just with a noun. The weak form is used after a demonstrative or a possessive pronoun.

Tab. 11: Old English Weak Adjectives

	masculine	neuter	feminine
	'the foolish king'	'the foolish child'	'the foolish woman'
nom. sg.	*se dola cyning*	*þæt dole bearn*	*sēo dole fæmne*
gen. sg.	*þæs dolan cyninges*	*þæs dolan bearnes*	*þære dolan fæmnan*
dat. sg.	*þæm dolan cyninge*	*þæm dolan bearne*	*þære dolan fæmnan*
acc. sg.	*þone dolan cyning*	*þæt dole bearn*	*þā dolan fæmnan*
inst. sg.	*þȳ dolan cyninge*	*þȳ dolan bearne*	–
nom. pl.	*þā dolan cyningas / bearn / fæmnan*		
gen. pl.	*þāra dolra (or dolena) cyninga / bearna / fæmnena*		
dat. pl.	*þæm dolum cyningum / bearnum / fæmnum*		
acc. pl.	*þā dolan cyningas / bearn / fæmnan*		

Tab. 12: Old English Strong Adjectives

	masculine	neuter	feminine
	'a foolish king'	'a foolish child'	'a foolish woman'
nom. sg.	*dol cyning*	*dol bearn*	*dolu fæmne*
gen sg.	*doles cyninges*	*doles bearnes*	*dolre fæmnan*
dat. sg.	*dolum cyninge*	*dolum bearne*	*dolre fæmnan*
acc. sg.	*dolne cyning*	*dol bearn*	*dole fæmnan*
inst. sg.	*dole cyninge*	*dole bearne*	–
nom. pl.	*dole cyningas*	*dolu bearn*	*dola fæmnan*
gen. pl.	*dolra cyninga / bearna / fæmnena*		
dat. pl.	*dolum cyningum / bearnum / fæmnum*		
acc. pl.	*dole cyningas*	*dolu bearn*	*dola fæmnan*

The comparative of adjectives was regularly formed by adding *-ra*, and the superlative by adding *-ost*. Characteristic endings of adverbs are *-e*, *-lice*, and *-unga*. Adverbs are normally compared by adding *-or* and *-ost*.

In Old English times the system of the personal pronouns was not much more complex than it is today except for the loss of the dual number and the old second person singular forms.

Tab. 13: Personal Pronouns

1st person	singular		dual	plural
nominative	*ic*	'I'	*wit* 'we both'	*wē* 'we all'
genitive	*mīn*	'my, mine'	*uncer* 'our(s) both'	*ūre* 'our(s) (all)'
dative	*mē*	'me'	*unc* 'us both'	*ūs* 'us all'
accusative				
2nd person	singular		dual	plural
nominative	*þū* 'you' (sg.)		*git* 'you both'	*gē* 'you all'
genitive	*þīn* 'your(s)' (sg.)		*incer* 'your(s) both'	*ēower* 'your(s) (all)'
dative	*þē* 'you' (sg.)		*inc* 'you both'	*ēow* 'you all'
accusative				
3rd person	masculine	feminine	neuter	plural
nominative	*hē* 'he'	*hēo* 'she'	*hit* 'it'	*hīe* 'they'
genitive	*his* 'his'	*hire* 'her(s)'	*his* 'its'	*hira / heora* 'their(s)'
dative	*him* 'him'	*hire* 'her'	*him* 'it'	*him, heom* 'them'
accusative	*hine* 'him'	*hīe* 'her'	*hit* 'it'	*hīe* 'them'

The Old English interrogative pronoun was *hwā* ('who') with its declined forms. The particle *þe* introduced a relative clause, often together with the forms of the demonstrative pronoun.

✍✍✍ Exercise 9: Old English Inflections[18]

Each italicized word in the sentences below contains a modern survival of one of the following Old English inflections:

A   nominative-accusative plural ending in -*as*
B   nominative-accusative plural ending in -*an*
C   nominative-accusative plural with mutation of the stem vowel
D   nominative-accusative plural identical with nominative-accusative singular
E   genitive singular ending in -*es*
F   nominative-accusative plural ending in -*ru*
G   genitive plural ending in -*a*

Match these modern forms with the Old English inflections listed above. (You may need to consult an etymological dictionary.)

1) The *boats* were floating by the dock.
2) He found a *raven's* nest.
3) They took a four-*day* trip.
4) The *oxen* follow the plow.

5) The *dormice* are hunting for food.
6) The *sheep* are in the pasture.
7) Suffer the little *children* to come unto me. (double plural)

4.2 Verbs

Old English verbs were either weak, adding a *-d* or a *-t* to form their past tense and past participles, or strong, showing a pattern of vowel change (called *gradation*) inherited from the Indo-European language.

Tab. 14: Old English Verbs – Strong Classes

class	rule	gradation series	infinitive	preterite singular	preterite plural	past participle
I	*ī* + 1 consonant	*ī ā i i*	*drīfan*	*drāf*	*drifon*	*drifen*
II	*ēo / ū* + 1 consonant	*ēo / ū ēa u o*	*crēopan*	*crēap*	*crupon*	*cropen*
III	*e* + 2 consonants	*e æ u o*	*berstan*	*bærst*	*burston*	*borsten*
IV	*e* + 1 consonant (*l/r*)	*e æ ǣ o*	*beran*	*bær*	*bǣron*	*boren*
V	*e* + 1 consonant (stop/fricative)	*e æ ǣ e*	*sprecan*	*spræc*	*sprǣcon*	*sprecen*
VI	*a* + 1 consonant	*a ō ō a*	*scacan*	*scōc*	*scōcon*	*scacen*
VII	preterite vowel *ēo/ē*	*ā ēo ēo ā* *ǣ e ē ǣ*	*cnāwan* *lǣtan*	*cnēow* *lēt*	*cnēowon* *lēton*	*cnāwen* *lǣten*

Verbs from all of the seven strong classes have survived in Present-day English, but sound change and analogy have caused changes within the gradation series of the strong verbs. Some common strong verbs in Present-day English include the following:

class   I: *bite, drive, glide, hide, ride, rise, shine, slide, stride, strike, write*
class   II: *choose, creep, fly, freeze*
class   III: *begin, bind, burst, fight, find, ring, run, sing, sink, spring, swim, wind*
class   IV: *bear, break, come, steal, swear, tear*
class   V: *eat, give, lie, see, sit, speak, weave*
class   VI: *draw, shake, stand, swear*
class VII: *beat, blow, fall, grow, hold, know, throw*

There are three classes of weak verbs in Old English. Most of the verbs of class I have an i-mutated vowel throughout the stem (see table 15). In addition, there are anomalous verbs, such as *bēon/wesan*, *dōn*, *gān*, and *willan*.

Tab. 15: Old English Verbs – Weak Classes

class	infinitive		preterite		past participle	
I	*fremman*	'to do'	*fremede*	'did'	*fremed*	'done'
	cēpan	'to keep'	*cēpte*	'kept'	*cēped/cēpt*	'kept'
	hȳran	'to hear'	*hīerde*	'heard'	*hīered*	'heard'
	ferian	'to carry'	*freed*	'carried'	*fered*	'carried'
	bycgan	'to buy'	*bohte*	'bought'	*both*	'bought'
	þencan	'to think'	*þōhte*	'thought'	*þōht*	'thought'
	þyncan	'to seem'	*þūhte*	'seemed'	*þūht*	'seemed'
II	*endian*	'to end'	*endode*	'ended'	*endod*	'ended'
III	*habban*	'to have'	*hæfde*	'had'	*hæfd*	'had'
	secgan	'to say'	*sægde*	'said'	*sægd*	'said'
	libban	'to live'	*lifde*	'lived'	*lifd*	'lived'

🖉🖉 Exercise 10: Strong and Weak Verbs

1) The following verbs are cited in both their infinitive and their preterite singular forms. Decide which are weak and which are strong.

A	*brengan*	*brohte*	'to bring'	F	*locian*	*locode*	'to look'
B	*gifan*	*geaf*	'to give'	G	*scinan*	*scan*	'shine'
C	*habban*	*hæfde*	'to have'	H	*steppan*	*stop*	'to step'
D	*hyran*	*hyrde*	'to hear'	I	*tæcan*	*tahte*	'to teach'
E	*hon*	*heng*	'to hang'	J	*hyngran*	*hygrede*	'to hunger'

Some Present-day English verbs come in pairs: *fall* and *fell*, *lie* and *lay*, *sit* and *set*.

2) What difference in meaning is there between the members of each pair?
3) What is the cause of their difference in form?
4) Which verb in each pair is weak, and which is strong?

4.3 Old English Word Order

Compared to Present-day English, the word order in Old English was relatively free. The relation of the words in a sentence was largely indicated by means of inflections. Thus Old English is a synthetic language, while Present-day English is an analytic language.[19] Accordingly in Old English, various word orders were possible, but there were certain patterns which were used most. The following sequences were common in Old English (see table 16).

As in Present-day English, the sequence 'subject + verb' can occur in both main and subordinate clauses. Whilst in subordinate clauses the order 'subject... + verb' is most common in Old English, the order 'verb + subject' is found in questions, certain positive and negative statements, and in subordinate clauses of condition and

Tab. 16: Old English Word Order

pattern	example[20]
subject + verb	*Hē hæfde rīce oð gemǣru Humbre strēames.* 'He had dominion up to the confines of the Humber river.'
	Ðā wæs æfter manigum dagum þæt sē cyning cōm tō þǣm ēalande. 'Then it was after many days that the king came to the island.'
subject... + verb	*ðā hē þā sē cyning þās word gehīerde* 'when the king heard these words'
	forþon hē crīsten wīf hæfde 'since he had a Christian wife'
verb + subject	*On þyssum ēalande cōm ūp sē Godes þēow Augustinus* [...]. 'On this island came up the servant of God, Augustine, [...].'
	Nāmon hīe ēac swelce him wealhstodas of Franclande mid. 'Took they likewise with them interpreters from Frank-land.'

concession. The radical changes in unstressed vowels and decay of inflections gradually led to the sequence 'subject + verb' as the main order in Present-day English.

✍ ✍ Exercise 11: Word Order

This is the entry from the *Peterborough Chronicle*[21] for AD 787 and its word for word translation (see next page).

1) Identify the clause elements and the order of the subjects and verbs in the main clauses above (S = subject, V = verb, O= object, A = adverbial).

2) Rewrite the word for word translation in normal contemporary English.

Hēr nam breohtric cining offan dohter ēadburge. ꝛ on his dagum cōmon ǣrest .iii. scipu norðmanna of hereða lande.ꝛ þā se gerēfa þǣr tō rād. ꝛ hē wolde drīfan tō ðes ciniges tūne þȳ hē nyste hwæt hī wǣron. ꝛ hine man ofslōh þā. Ðæt wǣron þā ǣrestan scipu deniscra manna þe angel cynnes land gesōhton.	Here took Beorhtric king Offa's daughter Eadburh. ꝛ in his days came first 3 ships of Northmen from Hörthaland.[22] ꝛ then the reeve there to rode. ꝛ he [them] wished drive to the king's manor for he knew not what they were. ꝛ him one slew then. That were the first ships of Danish men that English people's land sought.

5 Vocabulary

The vocabulary of Old English presents a mixed picture.[23] It was basically Germanic, with relatively few loanwords. Frequent use was made of compounds and derivations. Many Old English words have survived in Present-day English, for example *bītan* ('to bite'), *blōd* ('blood'), *ende* ('end'), *dæg* ('day'), *dohtor* ('daughter'), *drincan* ('drink'), *etan* ('eat'), *fæder* ('father'), *mōdor* ('mother'), *mōna* ('moon'), *niht* ('night'), *steorra* ('star'), *sumor* ('summer'), *sunne* ('sun'), *winter* ('winter'), and *wundor* ('wonder'). Many other Old English words have not survived at all: *blīcan* ('shine, gleam'), *cyme* ('arrival'), *lēan* ('reward'), or *wita* ('wise man'). Some have changed their meaning. Thus Old English *dēor* meant 'wild animal' rather than 'deer'. Similarly, *mōd* meant 'courage' not 'mood', *scēawian* 'see, look at' not 'show', and *tīd* 'time' not 'tide'. However, the English language was not merely the product of the dialects of the Germanic tribes who had settled in England. It was also brought into contact with the languages of the Celts, the Romans, and the Scandinavians.

5.1 Celtic Influence

The number of Celtic borrowings is extremely small. Apart from place names their influence is almost negligible. Within this small number one can distinguish two groups:

a) those learned through everyday contact with the natives:
   binn ('basket, crib'), *bratt* ('cloak'), *luh* ('lake'), *bannoc* ('a piece of a cake or a loaf'), and *brocc* ('badger'); and

b) those introduced by the Irish missionaries in the north:
   cross, *drȳ* ('magician'), and *clugge* ('bell').

Most of them soon died out. The extensive influence of Celtic loans can only be found in place names and rivers, for instance, *Avon, Cumberland, Dover, Kent, London, Thames*, and *York*.

5.2 Greek Loanwords

Almost all Greek words that were taken over in Old English times were indirect borrowings. They entered the English language through Latin. Examples for indirect borrowings are Present-day English *angel*, *church*, *demon*, *idol*, and *psalm* (see also 5.3). One of the few words that has been directly borrowed from Greek is *devil*.

5.3 Latin Influence

We can distinguish three spheres of Latin influence on Old English: a) continental borrowing, b) Latin through Celtic transmission, and c) the introduction of Christianity.

a) Continental Borrowing
   The earliest Latin borrowings owe their adoption to the early contact between the Romans and the Germanic tribes on the continent (several hundred Latin words). Words were taken over from the areas of warfare, agriculture, trade (wine), domestic life, and household. Examples are *camp* ('battle'), *cheap*, *cheese*, *mile*, *street*, and *wine*.

b) Latin through Celtic Transmission
   Before Christianization there was hardly an opportunity for direct contact between Latin and Old English in the British Isles; the Latin words that found their way into English during that time came through Celtic transmission. The Celts adopted about 600 Latin words, but only a handful of them survived. One of the most likely borrowings is the word *ceaster* ('camp'), as in *Worcester*, *Gloucester*, and *Lancaster*. Some other examples are the words *port*, *munt* ('mountain'), *torr* ('tower, rock'), and *wīc* ('village').

c) The Christianizing of Britain
   As a result of the conversion to Christianity and the establishment of the Church, many Latin words came into the language (about 450 words). The words that made their way into Old English can be divided into two groups:
   – words that were borrowed early on: *altar*, *candle*, *cap*, *deacon*, *disciple*, *elephant*, *fennel*, *pope*, *priest*, *pine* ('tree'), *psalm*, *shrine*, and
   – words adopted in the tenth and eleventh centuries, and often of a more learned character (related to the religious revival that accompanied the Benedictine reform): *accent*, *apostle*, *cancer*, *cantor*, *cedar*, *demon*, *history*, *paper*, *prophet*, *scorpion*, *title*. Many of these borrowings were used infrequently, and often they were later reintroduced into English via French.

5.4 Scandinavian Influence

The group of Scandinavian languages came from one parent language called Old Norse. It was cognate with Old English, as they both came from the same earlier Germanic languages. It seems very likely that Old English speakers and Old Norse speakers were able to understand each other. Old English borrowed almost 1000 words from Old Norse, which, however, in their majority are attested in written documents only in the Middle English period. Many loans are words of everyday life: *anger*, *bag*, *both*, *birth*, *bull*, *call*, *die*, *dirt*, *flat*, *get*, *gift*, *husband*, *ill*, *knife*, *leg*, *loose, same, sister, sky, steak, take, want, weak, window*, and many others. Even the personal pronouns *they, their*, and *them* were borrowed.

Present-day English words beginning with [sk] are clearly Scandinavian borrowings, for instance *sky, skin*, and *skill*. In Old English [sk] was early palatalized to [ʃ], written ⟨sc⟩. Thus we have *shirt* from Old English and *skirt* from Old Norse. Furthermore, the retention of the velar pronunciation of *k* and *g* in such words as *kid, get, give*, and *egg* is an indication of Scandinavian origin. Old English had [tʃ] or [j]: *child, chin, yard, yield.*

Last but not least there are over 1,500 Scandinavian place names in England, for instance, the place names ending in *-by* (meaning 'farm' or 'town' in Danish), as in *Whitby, Derby*, and *Rugby*. Other place names contain the Scandinavian word *thorp* ('village'), cf. *Althorp, Bishopsthorpe*, and *Linthorpe*; others end in *-toft* ('a piece of ground'): *Brimtoft, Eastoft*, and *Nortoft*. English families with names ending in *-son* have Scandinavian ancestors: *Davidson, Jackson*, and *Henderson*.

5.5 French Loanwords

French borrowings are not only due to the Norman conquest: They can be found in Old English, too. The Anglo-Saxons also had relations with France before the Conquest. In the 10th and 11th centuries, close contacts grew between France and England for political and religious reasons. From this time, a handful of French loanwords have survived, among them *clerc* ('clerk'), *prūd* ('proud'), *tūr* ('tower'), *castel* ('castle'), *prisun* ('prison'), and *market*. The French words of this period make up only about 0.3 percent of all borrowings – but today the French loans comprise about 60 percent of all borrowings!

✍ ✍ Exercise 12: Scandinavian Loanwords[24]

The following loanwords are borrowings from Old Norse that replaced native words in Late Old English or Early Middle English. Check each Present-day English form in the *Oxford English Dictionary* for the Old Norse word, the Old English word that it replaced, and the form that the Old English took if it survived into Middle or Present-day English.[25] Look up each word under the first entry for its part of speech – substantive (sb.), adjective (adj.), or verb (vb.) – as indicated below.

1) *bait* (vb.)	7) *loose* (adj.)	13) *swain* (sb.)
2) *call* (vb.)	8) *race* 'run' (sb.)	14) *weak* (adj.)
3) *cast* (vb.)	9) *raise* (vb)	15) *window* (sb.)
4) *get* (vb.)	10) *scab* (sb.)	
5) *high* (adj.)	11) *sister* (sb.)	
6) *loan* (sb.)	12) *skirt* (sb.)	

6 Additional Text Samples

Not much of the literature of Old English has survived until today. It is said that there are 30,000 verses of some prose texts left. Moreover, the existing texts which date back to around 1000 are not in their original version but have been copied. The earliest texts were supposedly written around the year 600 in monasteries.

There are four bigger collections from Old English that have survived until today: the Beowulf manuscripts, the Exeter Book, the Vercelli Book, and the Junius Book. Whereas all works of Old English are either in the Pagan / Germanic or the Christian tradition, the poems can be divided by subject matter. There are heroic poems (treating heroic subjects), historic poems (dealing with battles), religious poems (translations of the Testaments or poems on monks and saints), and other poems (elegies or riddles).

✍ Exercise 13: Lord's Prayer[26]

The following three translations of the Lord's Prayer correspond to the three major periods of the English language: Old English (or Anglo-Saxon), Middle English, and Early Modern English. Text A was written about the year 1000, text B is from the Wycliffe Bible of 1380, and text C is from the King James Bible of 1611.

A Old English:
Fæder ūre, þū þe eart on heofonum, sī þīn nama gehālgod. Tō becume þīn rīce. Gewurðe þīn willa on eorðan swā swā on heofonum. Ūrne gedæghwāmlican hlāf syle ūs tō dæg. And forgyf ūs ūre gyltas, swā swā wē forgyfað ūrum gyltendum. And ne gelǣd þū ūs on costnunge, ac ālȳs ūs of yfele. Sōðlīce.

B Middle English:
Oure fadir that art in heuenes halowid be thi name, thi kyngdom come to, be thi wile don in erthe as in heuene, yeue to us this day oure breed ouir other substaunce, & foryeue to us oure dettis, as we foryeuen to oure dettouris, & lede us not in to temptacion: but delyuer us from yuel, amen.

C Early Modern English:
Our father which art in heauen, hallowed be thy Name. Thy kingdome come. Thy will be done, in earth, as it is in heauen. Giue vs this day our dayly bread. And forgiue vs our debts, as we forgiue our debters. And leade vs not into temptation, but deliuer vs from euill: For thine is the kingdome, and the power, and the glory, for euer, Amen.

1) Which letters of the Old English writing system have been lost from the English alphabet?

2) At first sight, the letters *v* and *u* seem to be used arbitrarily in the King James translation, but there is a system in their use. Which is used at the beginning of a word? Which is used medially?

3) Which different forms does Old English have for the word *our*? Can you suggest why Old English has more than one form for this word?

4) List three phrases from the Wycliffe translation in which the use of prepositions differs from that in the King James version.

5) List three phrases from the Wycliffe translation in which the word order differs from that in the Old English version.

6) In general, does the Middle English version appear to be more similar to the Old English translation or to the King James translation? Give several reasons to support your answer.

🖎🖎🖎 Exercise 14: The Description of 'Scyld's Funeral Ship' from *Beowulf*

Translate lines 32 to 42 into Present-day English.[27] These words will assist you:

hȳð 'harbour', *standan* 'to stand', *stefn* 'prow' (German *Bug*), *īsig* 'icy' (German *glänzend, eisig*), *ūtfūs* 'eager to set out', *ālecgan* 'to lay down', *lēof* 'dear', *þēoden* 'lord, king', *bēag* 'ring', *brutta* 'distributor', *bearm* 'bosom', *mǣre* 'famous', *mādma* 'treasure', *feorweg* 'far away', *frætwe* 'precious things', *lǣdan* 'lead, bring', *cȳmlīcor* 'more nobly', *cēol* 'kiel' i.e. 'ship', *gyrwan* 'to equip', *hildewǣpen* 'war weapon', *heaðowǣd* 'war-dress, armour', *bil(l)* 'sword', *byrne* 'coat of mail' (German *Panzerhemd*), *licgan* 'to lie', *monig / mænig* 'a great many', *þā* (relative pronoun), *flōd* 'flood', *ǣht* 'possession', *gewītan* 'to go, depart'.

   þǣr æt hȳðe stōd hringedstefna
   īsig ond ūtfūs, æþelinges fær;
   ālēdon þā lēofne þēoden,
35 bēaga bryttan on bearm scipes,
   mǣrne be mǣste. Þǣr wæs mādma fela
   of feorwegum frætwa gelǣded;
   ne hȳrde ic cȳmlīcor cēol gegyrwan
   hildewǣpnum ond heaðowǣdum
40 billum ond byrnum; him on bearme læg
   mādma mænigo, þā him mid scoldon
   on flōdes ǣht feor gewītan.
   Nalæs hī hine lǣssan lācum tēodan,
   þēod-gestrēonum, þon þā dydon,
45 þē hine æt frumsceafte forð onsendon
   ǣnne ofer ȳðe umborwesende.
   þā gȳt hīe hīm āsetton segen g(yl)denne
   hēah ofer hēafod, lēton holm beran,
   gēafon on gārsecg; him wæs geōmor sefa,

50   murnende mōd.   Men ne cunnon
secgan to sōðe,   sele-rædende,
hæleð under heofenum, hwa þæm hlæste onfēng.

Here is the translation of lines 43 to 52:

No lesser gifts did they provide him
– the wealth of a nation – than those at his start
who set him adrift when only a child,
friendless and cold, alone on the waves.
High over his head his men also set
his standard, gold-flagged, then let the waves lap
gave him to the sea with grieving hearts
mourned deep in mind. Men cannot say,
wise men in hall nor warriors in the field,
not truly, who received that cargo.

Notes:

[1]   Taken from Crystal 1988: 156.

[2]   Taken from Freeborn [2]1998: 35.

[3]   Mercian and Northumbrian are often grouped together as Anglian.

[4]   Taken from Freeborn [2]1998: 37.

[5]   The most famous runic inscriptions in Britain appear on the Ruthwell Cross, near Dumfries, a monumental stone cross dating from the early eighth century. Another famous example is the runic inscription on a richly carved whalebone box, called the Franks Casket, now exhibited in the British Museum.

[6]   Adapted from Freeborn [2]1998: 34/35.

[7]   The word *anchorite* means 'religious hermit'.

[8]   Adapted from Freeborn [2]1998: 23.

[9]   In printing Old English texts today, long vowels are usually marked by a macron (¯).

[10]   The letters <g> and <w> are normally used for <ᣫ> and <ᵽ> in modern printed editions of Old English texts. Some grammars use a dot above the letters <c> and <g> to mark the palatal pronunciation.

[11]   This is not the standard German pronunciation but a regional variant (Rhineland).

[12] Taken from Sauer [2]1990: 16.

[13] For the complete text, see Baugh/Cable [4]1993: 60-62.

[14] Compare Lass 1987: 121-126 and Lass 1994: 41-71.

[15] Slighty adapted from Algeo [4]1993: 124/125.

[16] For a more detailed description of Old English grammar, see especially Campbell 1959: 222-351 and Mitchell/Robinson [5]1992: 17-54.

[17] The *n*-stem pattern is also called the weak declension, in contrast to the strong declension with stems originally ending in a vowel.

[18] Mainly based on Algeo [4]1993: 131.

[19] An analytic language is one that uses very few bound morphemes, its words being mostly one-syllable morphemes or compounds. An example of a highly analytic language is Chinese. By contrast, a synthetic language uses large numbers of bound morphemes, for instance inflectional suffixes. It often combines long strings of bound morphemes to form a single word. Examples of highly synthetic languages are Turkish and the Eskimo languages.

[20] The examples are taken from the Old English translation of Bede's *Ecclesiastical History* (the coming of the missionaries). For the complete text, see Baugh/Cable [4]1993: 60-62.

[21] Adapted from Freeborn [2]1998: 38.

[22] Around Hardanger Fjord.

[23] This chapter is mainly based on Baugh/Cable [4]1993: 72-100.

[24] Based on Cable [2]1993: 52.

[25] All the information that you need is in brackets at the beginning of each entry. In the *OED*, the abbreviation *a. ON* means 'adopted from Old Norse'.

[26] Slightly adapted from Algeo [4]1993: 15/16.

[27] Taken from *Beowulf and the Fight at Finnsburg*, edited by Klaeber [3]1950.

MIDDLE ENGLISH

1 The Norman Conquest

In 1066 the English king Edward the Confessor died childless, and Harold, son of the powerful Earl of Wessex, was elected king. Shortly afterwards, however, he was challenged by William, Duke of Normandy, who had been a second cousin to Edward. While Harold was fighting against another claimant to the throne in the north, William landed in the south. During the decisive battle of Hastings, Harold died and William put the English to flight. Soon after this, the Duke of Normandy ascended to the throne. In the following years he secured his position by erecting numerous castles. Furthermore, most of the English noblemen were killed and replaced by William's Norman followers. They became the ruling class – and they spoke French. Nevertheless, the language of the masses remained English.

2 The Dialectal Diversity of Middle English

As a consequence of the social and political turbulence brought about by the Norman conquest, the West Saxon standard system of spelling ceased to exist. Writers used spellings that matched the pronunciation of their dialect, and scribes sometimes changed the spelling of words according to their own dialect pronunciation. Today, we have a lot of evidence for the various Middle English dialects.

Basically, the dialectal areas of Old English remained the same, with the exception of the Mercian Midland of England, whose eastern and western part developed into two different dialectal areas. Thereafter, the five main dialects of Middle English were: Southern, Kentish, East Midlands, West Midlands, and Northern. Due to the dominance of French, none of the dialects were particularly prestigious, and no English standard developed until the decline of the language of the conquerors (see figure 10).

3 The Re-establishment of English

Until the 13th century, French remained the language of the upper classes in England. It was the language of government, law, administration, literature, and the Church, with Latin also used in documents as well as in scholarly and religious texts. The French spoke Norman French, a northern dialect of the language, which gradually developed characteristics of its own, and is now termed Anglo-Norman. English, though spoken by the majority of the population, was considered uncultivated and inferior. However, it seems that in the course of time, more and more French people became proficient in English, particularly churchmen, men of education, and those who had contact with the English on a regular basis.

Fig. 10: The Five Main Dialectal Areas of Middle English[1]

From the 13th century onwards, conditions changed in favor of English. There were several factors that contributed to the re-establishment of the language of the conquered people. In 1204, king John lost Normandy to the French crown. As a consequence, the Norman nobility had to break off its ties with its homeland and began to develop a national feeling towards England, which also raised the prestige of the English language. In addition, the Central French dialect of Paris had meanwhile become very prestigious in the rest of France, and the Anglo-Norman dialect was now considered rather backward and rustic. This fact contributed to the further isolation of the Anglo-Normans.

In the 14th century, the gap between England and France widened even more. In 1337, the Hundred Years' War broke out, and French became the language of the enemy. This time also saw the rise of an English middle class and, as an effect of the Black Death, the growing economic significance of the laboring class. In consequence, the English language continually gained importance. It began to be used in the law courts and in schools. In 1399, and for the first time since the Norman conquest, a king who spoke English as his mother tongue seized the throne.

At the beginning of the 15th century, English began to be accepted in official writing as well. Thus the establishment of English was finally complete.[2]

4 The New Standard English

The rise of the English language also saw the rise of a new written standard. It began to emerge during the 15th century, and was based on the East Midland dialect of Middle English, especially the dialect of London. The East Midland district was the largest and most populous of the major dialectal areas, and it occupied a middle position between the north and the south. Furthermore, it was an extremely important commercial, agricultural, and educational area. Oxford and Cambridge belong to this region. But above all, the East Midland dialect became the basis of London speech, and London was the political, commercial, and cultural center of the nation, besides being by far the largest city in England. The influence of the dialect was increased considerably by the introduction of printing in 1476. Moreover, the famous court poet Geoffrey Chaucer wrote in London English. By the end of the 15th century, this dialect had become the literary standard.

5 Spelling

The insular script of Old English was gradually replaced by the Norman style of handwriting, called *Carolingian minuscule*. Whereas in Old English the letters were curved, they now appeared as angular forms. Because of this it was difficult to tell how many strokes had been made when letters like ⟨m, n, v, w, i, u⟩ occurred together. This dilemma has been called the *minim problem*. It was mainly solved by substituting ⟨y⟩ for ⟨i⟩, ⟨o⟩ for ⟨u⟩, and ⟨v⟩ for ⟨u⟩ in front of ⟨n⟩. Apart from that, certain Old English letters were replaced, and a number of new consonant signs were introduced. In addition to these changes, the scribes in the king's employment used a handwriting called *Chancery hand* and introduced some more new spelling conventions. For instance, they wrote *such* instead of *sych* or *swich*, and *shall* and *should* instead of *shal* or *shul* and *sholde*. Eventually the letters of the alphabet achieved their modern English form.

The letters ⟨æ⟩, ⟨ð⟩, and ⟨þ⟩ were replaced by ⟨ea, a, e⟩, ⟨þ⟩ (later ⟨th⟩), and ⟨u, uu⟩ (later ⟨w⟩) respectively. The Old English grapheme ⟨ʒ⟩ was written ⟨g⟩ if pronounced as the velar plosive [g]. If pronounced [j], it was spelled ⟨y⟩.

The palatal fricative [ç] and the velar fricative [x] were represented by the digraph ⟨gh⟩. Furthermore, the French introduced the letters ⟨ch⟩ for [tʃ], ⟨ss, s, sch⟩ (later ⟨sh⟩) for [ʃ], ⟨c⟩ for [s], ⟨z⟩ for [z], and ⟨v⟩ for [v]; further ⟨ou⟩ for [uː], and ⟨ie⟩ for [eː]. See table 17 below for a summary of the new major spelling conventions.[3]

Tab. 17: Middle English Spelling Conventions[4]

Middle English vowels	Old English letters	Middle English examples
a) the minim problem		
⟨v, o⟩ [ʊ]	⟨u⟩	*vnder* 'under', *comen* 'come', *sonne* 'sun'
⟨y⟩ [ɪ, iː]	⟨i⟩	*coming* 'coming', *myhtes* 'might' (plural), *myn* 'mine'
b) others		
⟨u⟩ [ʏ] >[ɪ]	⟨y⟩	*sunne* 'sin'
⟨ou, ow⟩ [uː]	⟨u⟩	*oute* 'out', *hous* 'house', *thow* 'you'
⟨ie⟩ [eː]	⟨e⟩	*þief* 'thief', *chief* 'chief', *field* 'field'

Middle English consonants	Old English letters	Middle English examples
a) insular letters		
⟨th⟩ [ð, θ]	⟨ð⟩, ⟨þ⟩	*þe, the* 'the'
⟨u, uu⟩ > ⟨w⟩ [w]	⟨ƿ⟩	*uuenen* 'believe' (German 'wähnen'), *sua* 'so', *wat* 'what'
⟨g⟩ [g]	⟨ȝ⟩	*god* 'good', *dogge* 'dog', *gadering* 'gathering'
⟨y⟩ [j]	⟨ȝ⟩	*yong* 'young', *yer* 'year'
⟨gh⟩ [ç], [x]	⟨h⟩	*right* 'right', *broghte* 'brought'
⟨ȝ⟩ [s], [z]	⟨s⟩	*Godeȝ* 'God's', *ȝel* 'zeal'
b) other monographs		
⟨u⟩, ⟨v⟩ [v]	⟨f⟩	*loue* 'love', *over* 'over'
⟨k⟩ [k] in front of ⟨i, e, n, l⟩	⟨c⟩	*kniht* 'knight', *maken* 'make', *konnynge* 'cunning'
⟨c⟩ [s] in front of ⟨e⟩, ⟨i⟩	⟨s⟩	*certayn* 'certain', *cite* 'city'
c) other digraphs / trigraphs		
⟨ch⟩ [tʃ]	⟨c⟩	*child* 'child', *chirche* 'church'
⟨g⟩ [dʒ]	⟨cȝ⟩	*gentil, segge* 'human being'
⟨s, ss, sch, sh⟩ [ʃ]	⟨sc⟩	*ssipe, schippe, shippe* 'ship'
⟨wh⟩ [hw]	⟨hw⟩	*why* 'why', *wher* 'where', *what* 'what'
⟨qu⟩ [kw]	⟨cw⟩	*queen* 'queen', *quenchen* 'quench'

Furthermore, vowel quantity was expressed by:

a) the doubling of the corresponding letters in closed syllables, e.g. *feet* [feːt] ('feet'), *good* [goːd] ('good').

b) the doubling of consonantal letters (for short vowels), e.g. *butter* ('butter'), *commen* ('come').

c) a 'silent' *-e* in open syllables, e.g. *name* ['naːmə] ('name'). Frequently an *-e* was added although there was no etymological justification for it, e.g. Old English *com* (3rd person singular past tense) > Middle English *come* [koːm].

6 From Old English to Middle English: Phonology

The Middle English period was marked by crucial phonological changes in the English language. Some of them were the outcome of the Norman conquest and the following period; others can be traced back to Old English times. They mainly affected the length of the vowels and the loss or rise of diphthongs. Above all, the changes led to a complete reorganization of the vowel system.

From the 9th century onwards, the short stressed vowels were lengthened in front of certain consonant clusters, usually a liquid or a nasal followed by a voiced stop ([mb, nd, ld, rd]). As a countermovement, the stressed long vowels were shortened in closed syllables, that is before all consonant groups other than those which caused lengthening. In addition, long vowels were shortened in three-syllable words and when unstressed.

In Early Middle English, a further type of lengthening occurred, which is called *Open Syllable Lengthening*. It did not depend on following consonants but on the openness or closeness of syllables.[5] The short stressed vowels [a], [ɛ], and [ɔ] were lengthened and changed into [aː], [ɛː], and [ɔː] respectively.

Not only did lengthening and shortening occur side by side, but also monophthongization and diphthongization. In Late Old English, the diphthongal system was already simplified: The long diphthongs monophthongized by merging with the long vowels identical to their first elements; and the short diphthongs merged with the equivalent short vowels. Thus we see a development from [æɑ] to [ɛː] and from [eo] via [øː] to [eː]. This leaves us with a diphthong-free vowel system at the end of the Old English period.

However, a number of new diphthongs already began to emerge during the following period of transition. Firstly, postvocalic [j], [w], and [ɣ] were vocalized. The sound [j] changed into [ɪ], and both [w] and [ɣ] became [ʊ]. Secondly, short vowels in front of [ç] and [x] were diphthongized. Back vowels and [a] developed the off-glide [-ʊ], and front vowels the off-glide [-ɪ]. These various changes left us finally with the new diphthongs [ɛɪ, ɔɪ, ɪʊ, ɛʊ, ɔʊ, aʊ].[6]

Tab. 18: The Main Phonological Changes from Old English to Middle English

vowel quantity	examples
a) lengthening of short vowels before [mb, nd, 1d, rd] (except a following 3ʳᵈ consonant)	[ɪ] > [i:] in *bindan* 'bind', *milde* 'mild', *cild* 'child' [ɪ] in *cildru* 'children'
b) shortening of long vowels before all other consonant groups (= in closed syllables)	[o:] > [ɔ] in *sōfte* 'soft' [e:] > [ɛ] in *cēpte* 'kept' [i:] > [ɪ] in *wīsdōm*
c) shortening of long vowels in trisyllabic words	[a:] > [ɔ:] > [ɔ] in *hāligdæg* 'holiday'
d) shortening of unaccented vowels	[o:] > [ɔ] > ([ə]) in *tō* 'to'
e) open syllable lengthening	[ɔ] > [ɔ:] in *open* 'open' [ɑ] > [a:] in *talu* 'tale'

vowel quality	examples
a) unrounding of high back vowels[7]	[y:] > [i:] in *hȳdan* 'hide' [ʏ] > [ɪ] in *cyssan* 'kiss'
b) [æ] and [æ°] > [a]	*wæs* > *was* 'was', *sæt* > *sat* 'sat'
c) [ɑ:] > [ɔ:]	*stān* > *stoon* 'stone'
d) [æ:] > [ɛ:]	*clǣne* > *clene* 'small' (German *klein*)
e) leveling of unstressed vowels to [ə]	[ɔ] > [ə] in *macod* 'made' > *maked*

diphthongs	examples
a) monophthongization of diphthongs	[æɑ] > [ɛ:] in *hēap* 'heap' > *hepe* [eo] > [ø:] > [e:] in *hēold* 'hold' > *hēlde*
b) vocalization of [j] to [i] and [w, ɣ] to [u]	[æ] + [j] > [ɛɪ] in *said* *boga* ['bɔɣɑ] 'bow' > *bowe* ['bɔʊə] *nīwe* 'new' > *newe* [ɪʊ] *lagu* ('law' > *lawe* [aʊ]
c) diphthongization of vowels in front of [ç] and [x]	*hēah* ('high' > *hēh* [he:ç] > *heigh* [heɪç][8] *tāhte* 'thought' > *tahte* > *taughte* [taʊxtə]

consonants	examples
a) development of /v, z, ð/	*over* ['ɔ:vər] 'over' vs. *offren* ['ɔfrən] *zel* [zɛ:1] 'zeal' vs. *sele* [sɛ:1] 'seal'
b) [hn-], [h1-], and [hr-] merge with [n-], [1-], and [r-]	*hnutu* > *nute* 'nut' *hlēapan* > *lepen* 'leap'

There were also other qualitative changes that affected certain vowels. These were mainly: the unrounding of high back vowels; the lowering of [æ] to [a]; the raising of [ɑ:] to [ɔ:]; and the leveling of unstressed vowels into [ə], which gradually disappeared in final syllables.

The major development in the consonantal system was the rise of the new phonemes /v, z, ð/. In Old English, [v, z, ð] had been allophones of /f, s, θ/ occurring only in a voiced environment. Due to the loss of unstressed vowels in final syllables and the introduction of French loans, the allophones [v] and [z] achieved phonemic status. Initial [ð-] is the result of the voicing of [θ-] in unstressed words (such as *the*, *that*, *thus*). Furthermore, the initial consonant groups [hn], [hl], and [hr] were simplified to [n], [l], and [r].

The complex phonology of Middle English is made even more complicated by the difficult dialect situation. There were different pronunciations as well as different spellings of the same phoneme depending on the dialect area in which it appeared. Since our aim is to draw a coherent general picture, and because it is virtually impossible here to treat the dialectal differences adequately, we have mainly concentrated on London English.

7 Present-day English Spelling and Middle English Pronunciation

Due to the rise of a written standard and the introduction of printing, spelling became relatively stable in the 15th century, and it has stayed more or less the same until today. This means that modern English spelling reflects the state of the language of Late Middle English. However, pronunciation has changed significantly since then, and as a consequence certain letters today stand for a considerable number of different sounds and vice versa. Although Present-day English spelling is considered irregular, unpredictable, and even by some chaotic (there is no 1:1 relationship between one letter and one phoneme), it nevertheless follows discernible patterns. A knowledge of the historical developments helps us to understand the inconsistencies between Present-day English spelling and pronunciation. Furthermore, spelling today often provides the clue to the Middle English pronunciation. This is especially true for diphthongs and long vowels, which were affected most by later sound changes. The following table is intended to clarify the relationship between Present-day English spelling and Middle English pronunciation of some of the diphthongs and long vowels. [9]

The Middle English pronunciation of the given diphthongs and vowels either goes back to Old English or is related to the Anglo-Norman or French influence. For instance, the Middle English pronunciation [e:] of the spelling ⟨ie⟩ in *priest* is from Old English [eo], which changed into [ø:] and then into [e:]. But the Middle English pronunciation [e:] in words like *grief* and *chief* originates from Anglo-Norman.

Tab. 19: Present-day English and Middle English Pronunciation

PdE pronunciation[10]	PdE spelling	examples	ME pronunciation
[eɪ]	⟨a...e⟩	*tale, cradle, make*	[aː]
	⟨ay⟩, ⟨ai⟩	*day, main, nail, play*	[ɛɪ]
	⟨ei⟩, ⟨ey⟩	*vein, prey, reign, eight*	
[iː]	⟨ee⟩	*tree, feet, see*	[eː]
	⟨ea⟩	*cheap, dream, sea*	[ɛː]
	⟨ie⟩	*priest, thief, grief, chief, niece*	[eː]
[aɪ]	⟨i...e⟩, ⟨y⟩, ⟨i⟩	*time, blind, why*	[iː]
	⟨igh⟩	*right, fight, high*	[ɪç]
	⟨y⟩, ⟨ie⟩, ⟨ye⟩	*die, fly*	[iːə] > [iː]
[əʊ]	⟨o⟩	*stone, ghost, so*	[ɔː]
	⟨oa⟩	*road, loaf, boat*	[ɔː]
	⟨ou⟩, ⟨ow⟩	*soul, know*	[ɔʊ]
[uː]	⟨o⟩	*do, move, lose*	[oː]
	⟨oo⟩	*moon, tooth, cool*	[oː]
	⟨ou⟩	*group, soup*	[uː]
[aʊ]	⟨ou⟩	*loud, house, mouse*	[uː]
	⟨ow⟩	*town, cow, powder, fowl, bow* (vb)	[uː]

The pronunciation [ɔː] in Present-day English *stone* and *road* goes back to Old English [aː]. The Old English forms of Present-day English *soul* and *know* were *sāwol* and *cnāwan* respectively. The Middle English pronunciation [ɔʊ] is a result of the vocalization of [w]. The spelling in Present-day English *group*, *soup*, *town* and *powder* is influenced by French spelling. The Present-day English words *fowl* and *to bow* come from Old English *fugol* and *būgan* respectively (German 'Vogel', 'biegen'). Due to the vocalization of [ɣ], their stressed vowel was pronounced [uː] in Middle English.

Nevertheless, Present-day English spelling also shows historical irregularities. The spelling ⟨ea⟩ in *break*, *great* and *steak* was pronounced [ɛː] in Middle English but changed into [eː] and later into [eɪ] in Modern English (in analogy to Early Modern English *name* [nɛːm] > Present-day English [neɪm]). Present-day English *height* is spelled according to *high*. In words like *book*, *good* and *foot* Early Modern

English [u:] was shortened to [ʊ] (before [t], [d], [θ], [ð], [v], and [k] in monosyllabic words). But this shortening happened earlier in the words *blood* and *flood*, which both then took part in the Modern English development from [ʊ] to [ʌ]. This is why *book* is pronounced with a high and *flood* with a low short vowel.

🖎🖎 Exercise 15: Transcription of Middle English

Write these Middle English words in phonetic transcription. Unstressed *e* at the end of a word is phonetically [ə].

1)	*alone*	'alone'	9)	*doun, down*	'down'	17) *rode*	'road'
2)	*beten*	'beat'	10)	*doute*	'doubt'	18) *shoo*	'shoe'
3)	*biten*	'bite'	11)	*dreaden*	'dread'	19) *strete*	'street'
4)	*blame*	'blame'	12)	*faille*	'fail'	20) *top*	'top'
5)	*blood*	'blood'	13)	*flat*	'flat'	21) *wood*	'wood'
6)	*bothe*	'both'	14)	*fode*	'food'	22) *yelden*	'yield'
7)	*bright*	'bright'	15)	*love*	'love'		
8)	*doom*	'doom'	16)	*proceden*	'proceed'		

🖎🖎 Exercise 16: The Lengthening and Shortening of Vowels

Vowels were lengthened during the Late Old English period or in Early Middle English times:

A in front of [mb], [nd], [ld], [rd],
B in open syllables.

They were shortened:

C before all consonant groups other than [mb], [nd], [ld], [rd],
D in three-syllable words, and
E when unstressed.

Which of the five conditions listed above accounts for the vowel length of the first syllable in each of the following Middle English words?

1)	*aker*	'acre'	9)	*fifteen*	'fifteen'	16) *sutherne*	'southern'
2)	*beren*	'to bear'	10)	*finden*	'find'	17) *tale*	'tale'
3)	*bever*	'beaver'	11)	*ground*	'ground'	18) *today*	'today'
4)	*blosme*	'blossom'	12)	*holden*	'to hold'	19) *us*	'us'
5)	*cold*	'cold'	13)	*hope*	'hope'	20) *wepenes*	'weapons'
6)	*dore*	'door'	14)	*kinde*	'kind'	21) *wimmen*	'women'
7)	*fedde*	'fed'	15)	*naddre*	'adder'	22) *womb*	'womb'
8)	*feeld*	'field'					

8 Grammar

Whereas Old English was relatively highly inflected, Middle English developed into a language with few inflectional distinctions. Thus English changed from a more synthetic to a more analytic language. The simplification of inflections was supported by the reduction and loss of unstressed syllables at the end of words. This took place more quickly in the Northern and Midland dialects spoken in or close to the Danelaw area.[11] The English and Scandinavian words were often sufficiently similar to be comprehensible, but their inflectional endings differed. This may have contributed to the simplification of the inflectional system that generally happens when people speaking similar languages communicate together. In addition, the tendency of the leveling of cases can already be observed in Early Old English texts, and was thus also an inherent trend in Germanic and Old English. Furthermore, the influence of French contributed to the loss of endings as well. The leveling of inflections led to a greater reliance on word order and the more frequent and regular use of prepositions to show the meanings that were formerly expressed by inflections. Nevertheless, due to regional variance, there was a great deal of dialectal diversity in the remaining Middle English forms.

8.1 Nouns

The Old English noun endings -a, -u, and -e all became Middle English -e. In addition, more and more nouns began to move from other declensions into the a-stem type. The -as nominative-accusative plural and the -es genitive singular of this declension became the models for the plural and the genitive singular of most nouns.

Tab. 20: Nominal Inflections in Middle English

singular: nominative, accusative, and dative	*hous*
singular: genitive	*hous(e)s*
plural	*hous(e)s*

In Early Middle English, there were basically two possible ways of indicating the plural: the -s or -es from the strong declension of the a-stems, and the -en from the weak declension. The south favored -en, while -s or -es was more popular in the northern dialects. As we can deduce from the plural ending today, the latter form also spread to the south, and was finally accepted all over England in the course of the 14th century. Only a small number of words with the formerly weak plural ending -en have survived until today (*oxen, children, brethren*). Further relics of other declensions are the mutated plurals without an ending (*feet, geese, mice*), and the uninflected plurals (*deer, sheep*), which were neuter nouns in Old English. By the beginning of the Middle English period, three systems of nominal inflections had evolved, which in the course of time merged into the types as shown in table 20 above.

Grammatical gender was lost. This development started in the north during the 10th century and was completed in the south in the 13th century.

8.2 Pronouns

In contrast to the other word classes, the pronouns retained a considerable degree of complexity (and still do). Except for the neuter pronouns (*h*)*it*, *that*, *this*, and *what*, they preserved distinctive subject and object case forms. The dual number of the personal pronouns disappeared. The developments of the plural forms were mainly due to Scandinavian influence. The new personal pronoun *she* (formerly *hēo*) is believed to have been influenced by the demonstrative *sēo*. Table 21 gives a list of the personal and possessive pronouns.

Tab. 21: Personal and Possessive Pronouns

	1st person	2nd person	3rd person		
nom. sg.	*I*	*thou*	*he*	*she*	*hit*
gen. sg.	*my, myn*[12]	*thy, thyn*[12]	*his*	*hir (e)*	*his*
dat. sg.	*me*	*thee*	*him*	*hir (e)*	*him*
acc. sg.	*me*	*thee*	*him*	*hir*	*hit*
nom. pl.	*we*	*ye*	*they*		
gen. pl.	*oure*	*youre*	*hir*		
dat. pl.	*us*	*yow*	*hem*		
acc. pl.	*us*	*yow*	*hem*		

The demonstrative pronouns were reduced to *the*, *that*, and plural *tho*. The form *the* came to be used as an invariable definite article, with *that* and *tho* being left for the demonstrative function. The pronoun *tho* later gave way to *þās*, Present-day English *those*. The demonstrative *þēos*, *þēs*, and *þis* (*this*) were reduced to one singular form *þis*. The plural was formed by adding -*e* to the singular (-*e* was the ending of the plural of adjectives), which gives us the form *thise* or *thēse* (*these*). We thus arrive at the Present-day English pronouns *that* – *those* and *this* – *these*.

The Old English masculine-feminine interrogative pronoun *hwā* became *who* and the neuter form *hwæt* became *what*. As with the other pronouns, the dative *whom* replaced the accusative and was now used in any objective function. The genitive *whos* was formed by adding the ending -*s* from the original genitive form *hwæs* to the nominative masculine-feminine *who*. From the 14th century onwards, the interrogative pronouns were also used as relative pronouns (plural *which*, genitive *whos*, accusative *whom*). The usual relative pronoun in Middle English was *that*. All these pronouns are still in use today.

8.3 Adjectives

In both the strong and weak declensions of the adjective, the form of the nominative singular was extended at an early stage to all cases of the singular, and that of the nominative plural to all cases of the plural. The result was that only two forms remained: the base-form without an ending and a form with the ending -e which was used both for the plural and as the weak form:

Tab. 22: Strong and Weak Forms of the Adjective

	strong	weak
singular	*yong* 'young'	*yonge*
plural	*yonge*	*yonge*

When the final -e was lost towards the end of the Middle English period, these two forms became the same, and the adjective became undeclinable, as it is today.

8.4 Verbs

The older verbal endings -an, -ian, and -en all fell together as -en. With the later loss of final inflectional -n in some of these forms, only -e [-ə] remained and was soon to disappear, too. This fact explains the uninflected infinitives, preterite plurals, and some past participles of strong verbs in Present-day English, as, for instance:

Tab. 23: Verb Forms

	Old English	Middle English	Present-day English
infinitive	*findan*	*finden*	*find*
preterite plural	*fundon*	*founde(n)*	*found*
past participle	*funden*	*founde(n)*	*found*

Apart from the reduction and loss of the verbal inflections, the loss of strong verbs was most significant. Nearly a third of the strong verbs in Old English seem to have died out in Early Middle English, and others were to follow. Furthermore, due to analogy, many strong verbs developed weak forms. The large group of weak verbs with *d* or *t* in the suffix of the preterite and past participle offered a consistent pattern of analogy for the shrinking number of strong verbs. The surviving strong verbs underwent further leveling and analogical influence. Today only about 60 strong verbs remain in the English language (out of about 270 attested in Old English). A few verbs even maintain both a weak and a strong form, for instance *hang – hung / hanged, weave – wove / weaved*.

The ending of the present participle began to be changed from -nd to -ing. The *ing*-ending came from the Old English verbal noun ending -*ung*, as in Old English *offrung* ('offering'). In the 14th century the new form extended from the southwest to London, Kent, and the Midlands. Moreover, past participles that had been marked with the prefix *ge-* in Old English started to occur without it. The alternative forms were now used side by side, for instance *herd* and *y-herd* ('[I have] heard').

✍ Exercise 17: Middle English Personal Pronouns[13]

Translate the following sentences from Chaucer and insert the pronouns. Person, number, gender, and case are provided.

1) *And in* __ (3rd person singular masculine genitive) *gentil herte he thoughte anon* ('immediately').
2) *How myghty and how greet a lord is* __ (3rd person singular masculine nominative)!
3) *And he* __ (3rd person plural dative) *graunteth* ('grants') *grace, and thus he seyde*.
4) *Though that* __ (3rd person singular feminine nominative) *were a queene or a princesse*.
5) __ (2nd person singular genitive) *temple wol* __ (1st person singular nominative) *worshipe everemo* ('evermore').
6) *As keep me fro* __ (2nd person singular genitive) *vengeaunce and* __ (2nd person singular genitive) *ire*.
7) __ (1st person singular nominative) *am*, __ (2nd person singular nominative) *woost* ('know'), *yet of thy compaignye*.
8) *Now help* __ (1st person singular accusative), *lady, sith* ('since') __ (2nd person plural nominative) *may and kan*.
9) __ (2nd person singular nominative) *shalt ben wedded unto oon* ('one') *of tho* ('those').
10) *Yif* ('give') __ (1st person singular dative) *the victorie*, __ (1st person singular nominative) *aske* __ (2nd person singular accusative) *namoore* ('no more').

✍ Exercise 18: Strong and Weak Verbs in Middle English[14]

Chaucer alternated between the strong and weak forms for the past tense and past participle in some verbs. Identify the verb forms from Chaucer below as strong or weak.

1) *He* walked *in the feeldes, for to prye* ('gaze').
2) *That in a forest faste he* welk *to wepe*.
3) *Therwith he* weep *that pitee was to heere*.
4) *But soore* ('sorely') wepte *she if oon* ('one') *of hem* ('them') *were deed*.
5) *This Pompeus, this noble governour, Of Rome, which* ('who') *that* fleigh *at this bataille* ('battle').
6) *He* fledde *awey for verray* ('true') *sorwe* ('sorrow') *and shame*
7) *For joye him thoughte he* clawed ('patted') *him on the bak*.

8)   *With that aboute y* clew ('scratched') *myn hed.*

9)   *But for the moore* ('greater') *part they* loughe *and pleyde.*

10)   *For he had* lawghed, *had he loured* ('frowned').

9 Vocabulary

While the French language did not have much influence on the structure of the English language (except for phonology and orthography), it had a far-reaching effect on its vocabulary. French words were borrowed in large numbers. It has been estimated that the number of French words that came into the English language in the Middle English period was over ten thousand, and of these about 75 percent are said to be still in current use. In the 11th and 12th centuries the number of French loanwords was still rather small. But with the rising prestige of English, the French upper classes adopted the language of the common people and carried over many French words into the re-established English language. These words had largely to do with government and administration, but they also included many common words. This happened in the 13th century, and even more so in the 14th century.

Many French words replaced an Old English equivalent, and hundreds of Old English words were lost, but at the same time, Old English and French words often survived side by side. They developed different connotations or stylistic levels and became synonyms. Examples are *to deem* ('to consider', formal use) and *to judge* ('to assess'); *hearty* ('loud, cheerful') and *cordial* ('warm, friendly'); *house* ('residential building') and *mansion* ('large, impressive house'); *stench* ('very unpleasant smell'), *smell* ('odor', of unknown origin), and *scent* ('pleasant smell'). The French borrowings were often associated with literature. An interesting case are the words for some animals and their meat. From the beginning, the original French words of *beef, mutton, pork,* and *veal* were used for the meat, while the Anglo-Saxon words *cow, sheep, pig,* and *calf* remained expressions for the living animals.

Since the French words came into English from two dialects of French, Anglo-Norman (the Norman spoken in English), and Central French (the French of Paris, later Standard French), we find some *doublets* in the English language today. The initial sequences [ga] and [ka] became [dʒa] and [tʃa] in Central French, but stayed the same in Norman French. In addition, Old French [s] had become [tʃ] in Normandy. This gives us the pairs *catch – chase,* and *cattle – chattle.* The first word of both pairs originates from the Norman dialect, the latter from Central French. Another example is the avoidance of initial [w] in Central French but not in Anglo-Norman. This difference can be seen in the doublets *wage – gage* ('pledge'), *warden – guardian,* and *warranty – guarantee.* On the whole, however, only the early French loanwords were taken from Norman. Central French had become fashionable in the 13th and 14th centuries, and most words were borrowed from this dialect. Sometimes the same French word was even borrowed at various periods in the history of English. For instance, *gentle* ('calm, kind') was borrowed in the 13th century, *genteel* ('well-bred, refined') and *jaunty* ('confident, energetic') in the 17th century.

During the 14th and 15th centuries, several words also came into the language directly from Latin. Most of these words were scholarly terms and belonged to such fields as religion, medicine, law, and literature. They were often associated with an elevated style of writing. The simultaneous borrowing of French and Latin sometimes resulted in synonyms. Common examples are: *ask* (Old English) – *question* (French) – *interrogate* (Latin); *kingly* – *royal* – *regal*; *rise* – *mount* – *ascend*; *time* – *age* – *epoch*. The Old English word is usually the more general one, with the French word more formal, and the Latin word more technical.

Tab. 24: Summary of Vocabulary Influences

language	fields	examples
French	governmental and administrative words	*government, state, empire, nobility, baron, duke*
	ecclesiastical words	*religion, prayer, clergy, friar, saint, mercy*
	law	*justice, crime, punishment, prison, property, heritage*
	army and navy	*armor, battle, castle, tower, war, sergeant*
	fashion, meals, and social life	*fashion, dress, coat; poultry, toast, salad; couch, chair, lamp*
	art, learning, and medicine	*art, painting, music, beauty; study, logic, grammar, noun; physician, pain, stomach*
Latin	technical	*individual, prosecute, scripture, testify*
Flemish, Dutch, Low German		*dollar, landscape, cookie, easel*

In addition, there were other languages that brought new words into the English language at this time. Apart from a few Scandinavian and Celtic words, the new items came from the Low Countries, i.e. from Flemish, Dutch, and Low German. Since the Norman conquest there had been much contact with these countries, resulting from commercial and maritime links, not to mention William the Conqueror's Flemish wife. A small number of words were also borrowed from Spanish, Portuguese, Russian, and Arabic, mostly via French.[15]

As a result of this enormous number of loanwords, the English language changed considerably. Its Germanic character and its relatedness to the other Germanic languages was lost to a great extent. Many Old English words died out, and with them the ability to coin new words from native elements. Many Old English prefixes and suffixes fell out of use. In addition, the accentual patterns changed; but above all, the loanwords paved the way for future Greek and Latin borrowings that were to come into the English language during the Renaissance. This development was mainly caused by the formal similarity of French and Latin words. In some cases the similarity is so astonishing that we do not know whether a word has been borrowed from either French or Latin.

10 Text Samples

✍ Exercise 19: The Peterborough Chronicle[16]

The Peterborough Chronicle is a sequel to the Anglo-Saxon Chronicle which continued to be written at the monastery of Peterborough until 1154. It gives us the first immediate documentation of the modification in the language that had taken place by the middle of the 12th century. The following text is part of the annal for 1140.

> .mc.xl. On þis gær wolde þe king Stephne tæcen Rodbert eorl
> of gloucestre þe kinges sune Henries. ac he ne mythe for he
> wart it war. þer efter in þe lengten þestrede þe sunne ꝛ te
> dæi. abuton nontid dæies. þa men eten. ð me lihtede candles
> to æten bi ... wæron men suythe of wundred...
> þer efter wæx suythe micel uuerre betuyx þe king ꝛ Randolf
> eorl of cæstre noht for þi ð he ne iaf im al ð he cuthe axen
> him. alse he dide all othre. oc æfre þe mare he iaf heom. þe
> wærse he wæron him. þe eorl heold lincol agænes þe king ꝛ
> benam him al ð he ahte to hauen. ꝛ te king for þider ꝛ
> besætte him ꝛ his brother Willelm de Romare in þe castel. ꝛ
> te æorl stæl ut ꝛ ferde efter Rodbert eorl of gloucestre. ꝛ
> brohte him þider mid micel ferd. ꝛ fuhten suythe on
> Candelmasse dæi agenes heore lauerd. ꝛ namen him for his men
> him suyken ꝛ flugæn. ꝛ læd him to Bristowe ꝛ diden þar in
> prisun ꝛ in feteres. þa was al Engleland styred mar þan ær
> wæs. ꝛ al yuel wæs in lande...
> þa ferde Eustace þe kinges sune to france ꝛ nam þe kinges
> suster of france to wife. wende to bigæton normandi þæþurh.
> oc he spedde litel ꝛ be gode rihte for he was an yuel man.
> for ware se he com he dide mar yuel þanne god. he reuede þe
> landes ꝛ læide micele geldes on. He brohte his wif to
> engleland. ꝛ dide hire in þe castel in cantebyri. God wimman
> scæ wæs. oc scæ hedde litel blisse mid him. ꝛ Crist ne wolde
> ð he sculde lange rixan. ꝛ wærd ded ꝛ his moder beien...

Use this list of words to write a translation of the last section into Present-day English: *ferde* 'went', *sune* 'son', *wende* 'he hoped', *bigæton* 'obtain', *oc* 'but', *yuel* 'evil', *reuede* 'robbed', *micele* 'great', *geldes* 'taxes', *dide* 'put', *cantebyri* 'Canterbury', *scæ* 'she', *wolde* 'wished', *ð* 'that', *sculde* 'should', *rixan* 'reign', *beien* 'both'.

✍ ✍ Exercise 20: *Piers Plowman*

William Langland's *Piers Plowman* is one of the most famous medieval poems. It is written in the West Midland dialect. The following excerpt is the prologue of *Piers Plowman*, in which the writer has a dream.[17]

> In a somur sesoun whan softe was þe sonne
> Y shope me into shroudes as y a shep were;
> In abite as an heremite, vnholy of werkes,
> Wente forth in þe world wondres to here,
> And say many sellies and selkouthe thynges.
> Ac on a May mornyng on Maluerne hulles
> Me biful for to slepe, for werynesse of-walked;
> And in a launde as y lay, lened y and slepte,
> And merueylousliche me mette, as y may telle.
> Al þe welthe of the world and þe wo bothe
> Wynkyng, as hit were, witterliche y sigh hit;
> Of treuthe and tricherye, tresoun and gyle,
> Al y say slepynge, as y shal telle.
> Estward y beheld aftir þe sonne
> And say a tour – as y trowed, Treuthe was there-ynne.
> Westward y waytede in a while aftir
> And seigh a depe dale – Deth, as y leue,
> Woned in tho wones, and wikkede spiritus.
> A fair feld ful of folk fond y þer bytwene
> Of alle manere men, þe mene and þe pore,
> Worchyng and wandrying as þis world ascuth...

Try to translate the beginning of the text (*In a somur ...telle.*) with the help of the following vocabulary: *y* 'I', *shope* 'dressed', *shroudes* 'woollen clothes', *abite* 'habit, attire', *heremite* 'hermit', *say* 'saw', *sellies* 'marvels', *selkouthe* 'strange, marvelous', *ac* 'but', *hulles* 'hills', *biful* 'befell, happened', *of-walked* 'tired out', *launde* 'field', *lened* 'leaned, rested', *merueylousliche* 'marvelously', *mette* 'dreamed'.

Describe some of the linguistic features of the Middle English dialect (from the evidence provided in the text) under the following headings:

1) spelling conventions
2) evidence of pronunciation changes from Old English
3) pronoun forms
4) noun and verb inflections

5) grammatical structures and word order
6) sources of vocabulary

✍ ✍ Exercise 21: Geoffrey Chaucer's Prologue to the *Canterbury Tales*

Geoffrey Chaucer (circa 1340-1400) is considered to have been the greatest Middle English poet. He grew up in London as a son of a vintner, who kept strong contacts with the royalty. As a diplomat at court, he undertook several journeys to France and Italy, writing romances and poems in his free time. He was strongly influenced by the tradition of courtly literature. His best known work is the *Canterbury Tales*, the prologue of which gives us a portrait of contemporary characters. These people are on a pilgrimage to Canterbury and, in order to pass the time, they tell each other stories, which constitute the main part of the *Canterbury Tales*. Chaucer wrote in the London dialect of the Middle English of his time. The following excerpt is the beginning of the *General Prologue*:[18]

> Whan that Aprill with his shoures soote
> The droghte of March hath perced to the roote,
> And bathed every veyne in swich licour
> Of which vertu engendred is the flour;
> Whan Zephirus eek with his sweete breeth
> Inspired hath in every holt and heeth
> The tendre croppes, and the yonge sonne
> Hath in the Ram his halve cours yronne,
> And smale foweles maken melodye,
> That slepen al the nyght with open ye,
> (So priketh hem nature in hir corages);
> Thanne longen folk to goon on pilgrimages,
> And palmeres for to seken straunge strondes,
> To ferne halwes, kowthe in sondry londes;
> And specially from every shires ende
> Of Engelond to Caunterbury they wende,
> The hooly blisful martir for to seke,
> That hem hath holpen, whan that they were seeke.

1) Translate the text. The following words will assist you: *soote* 'mild, sweet', *of which vertu* 'by virtue of which', *Zephirus* 'Zephir, God of Wind', *eek* 'also', *holt* 'copse, spinney, grove', *croppes* 'shoots', *Ram* 'Aries', (*his*) *halve cours* 'halfway through', *priketh* 'stirs up', *corages* 'feelings, emotions', *thanne* 'then', *palmeres* 'pilgrims', *halwes* 'saints', *kowthe* 'well known, famous', *sondry* 'various, many'.

2) Give the Middle English and Present-day English pronunciation of *droghte, rote, yonge, open, corages*. After you have read chapter 2 in the Early Modern English section: Explain the sound changes from Middle English to Present-day English.

3) Give two examples from the text of the so-called *minim-problem*.

4) After you have read chapter 2 in the Early Modern English section: In Present-day English, *breeth* would not rhyme with *heeth* any more. What must have been the reasons for their different sound changes?

5) Give two examples of each of the following lexical changes: French borrowing, loss of words (Middle English > Present-day English), and meaning shift (Middle English > Present-day English).

Notes:

[1] The figure is taken from Freeborn [2]1998: 164.

[2] For a more thorough description of the socio-cultural background, see especially Baugh/Cable [4]1993: 124-153 and Leith 1983: 5-57.

[3] Old and new conventions often existed side by side.

[4] Summarized after Mossé [3]1986: 28-32.

[5] A syllable is closed if it ends in a consonant, c.f. *bit, lead, drin-king*. It is open if it ends in a vowel, c.f. *see, ba-ker, lea-der.*

[6] With the transcription [ɛɪ] instead of [aɪ] as in many other descriptions, I followed Obst/Schleburg 1999: 31.

[7] In West Saxon, the unrounding of [œ] to [ɛ] and [ø:] to [e:] had already taken place during the Old English period.

[8] The word [heɪç] developed further into [hi:ç].

[9] This overview is mainly based on Gimson/Cruttenden [5]1994: 88-137, Faiß 1989: 24-108, Moessner/Schaefer [2]1987: 72-90, and Obst/Schleburg 1999: 66-81.

[10] In *Received Pronunciation.*

[11] In Old English times, the area north of the line running roughly from Chester to London was governed by the Danes and was subject to Danish law.

[12] Before nouns beginning with a consonant, *my* and *thy* are used; before nouns beginning with a vowel, *myn* and *thyn.*

[13] Based on Cable [2]1993: 73-75.

[14] Based on Cable [2]1993: 75.

[15] For an extensive overview of Middle English vocabulary, see Baugh/Cable [4]1993: 163-184.

[16] Taken from Freeborn [2]1998: 83.

[17] Taken from *Piers Plowman by William Langland*, edited by Pearsall 1978.

[18] Taken from *The Works of Geoffrey Chaucer*, edited by Robinson [2]1976.

EARLY MODERN ENGLISH

The English language since 1500 is called Modern English. It can be further subdivided into Early Modern English (1500-1700), Late Modern English (1700-1900), and Present-day English (1900-today). Our focus in this chapter is on Early Modern English, but the developments from this period of time up to now will also be considered.

The Early Modern English period belongs to the era of the Renaissance. It saw the revival of learning and a renewed interest in the classical languages and literatures. Although English had already become the language of government, church, and education, the discussion still continued as to whether Latin suited the purposes of scholarship better. Translations from Latin into English in particular caused many problems and revealed that English was in need of new vocabulary, which was then borrowed from other languages. This period also witnessed the first efforts to regularize and preserve the English language. Since school education spread rapidly and literacy became much more common, there was a need for texts and reference books. School teachers and other learned men, sometimes even poets, were concerned about the state of the language in Britain and abroad. In the 16th and 17th centuries, the first spelling books, grammar books, and dictionaries were published, but it was only in the 2nd half of the 18th century that the standardization of the language reached its climax. By that time the English language had already taken on the shape it still has today.

1 Spelling and Pronunciation

When William Caxton introduced printing in England in 1476, he had to commit himself to a certain system of spelling, and he chose the spelling as used in the London area. As a result, a number of widely accepted spelling conventions developed which have lasted until today. In fact, spelling looked more or less the same in the 17th century as it does now. Nevertheless, there was still considerable variation in the written language. The spelling of the newly borrowed words had also to be standardized. Moreover, learned writers changed the spelling of a word according to its etymology. Sometimes letters were inserted although they were not pronounced, such as ⟨b⟩ in *debt* or *doubt*, because the corresponding words in Latin were so spelled (Latin *dēbitum*, *dubitāre*). In other instances the spelling of words was brought into line with others, for example, ⟨gh⟩ was inserted in *delight*, by analogy with *night* and *light*. Most significantly, the pronunciation continued changing, which increased the discontent over spelling.

It is therefore not surprising that several attempts were made to improve the spelling system. People saw that the letters of the alphabet were too few to match the sounds of English, and that the spelling of many words did not match their pronunciation. In the 16th century, a number of learned men wrote treatises on the English spelling system in an attempt to simplify it and to assign certain letters to certain sounds. Some more noteworthy examples are John Hart's *Orthographie* (1569), William Bullokar's *Booke at Large, for the Amendment of Orthographie for English Speech* (1580), and Richard Mulcaster's *Elementarie* (1582). Whilst the influence of these treatises remains debatable, credit is due to Samuel Johnson (1709-1784) and Noah Webster (1758-1843) who, by means of their dictionaries, finally settled the open questions on matters of spelling.[1]

✍ Exercise 22: John Hart's *Orthographie*[2]

One of the earliest books that advocated a reform of English spelling was John Hart's *Orthographie*, published in 1569. Here is a facsimile of the first two pages of the second part of the book, which is printed in Hart's new spelling; the transcription into Present-day English spelling follows below.

An exercise of that which is said: wherein is declared, how the rest of the consonants are made by th'instruments of the mouth: which was omitted in the premisses, for that we did not much abuse them. Chapter vii

In this title above-written, I consider of the ⟨i⟩ in exercise, & of the ⟨u⟩, in instruments: the like of the ⟨i⟩, in title, which the common man, and many learned, do sound in the diphthongs ⟨ei⟩, and ⟨iu⟩: yet I would not think it meet to write them, in those and like words, where the sound of the vowel only, may be as well allowed in our speech, as that of the diphthong used of the rude: and so far I allow observation for derivations. ∼ / Whereby you may perceive, that our single sounding and use of letters, may in process of time, bring our whole nation to one certain, perfet and general speaking. ∼ / Wherein she must be ruled by the learned from time to time. ∼ / And I can not blame any man to think this manner of new writing strange, for I do confess it is strange to my self, though before

I have ended the writing, and you the reading of this book, I doubt not but you and I shall think our labours well bestowed. ∼ / And not-with-standing that I have devised this new manner of writing for our /English, I mean not that /Latin should be written in these letters, no more then the /Greek or /Hebrew, neither would I write t'any man of any strange nation in these letters, but whenas I would write /English. ∼ / And as I would gladly counterfeit his speech with my tongue, so would I his writing with my hand. ∼ / Yet who could let me t'use my pen the best I could, thereby t' attain the sooner to the perfect pronunciation, of any strange speech: but writing /English, we may (as is said) use for every strange word, the same marks or letters of the voices which we do find in speech, without any other regard to show by writing whence the word is borrowed, then as we do in speaking. ∼ / For such curiosity in superfluous letters, for derivation or for difference, and so forth, is the disordering and confounding, of any writing: contrary to the law of the perfection thereof, and against all reason: whereby, it should be obedient unto the pronunciation, as to her lady and mistress: and so, add or diminish as she shall in success of time command.

Hart apparently believed that a reformed spelling, in which there was only one letter for each sound, would in time put an end to social and regional dialectal accents, and "bring our hol nasion tu on serten, perfet, and general speking". Believing that writing "Suld bi obedient untu de pronunsiasion", he sets out some of his objections to the current spelling system:

a) superfluous letters - some letters of the Roman alphabet are redundant and could be dropped,
b) adaptation - once a borrowing is assimilated, the English spelling should be used,
c) difference - words that are pronounced alike should not have a different spelling.

1) Give some examples of these 'abuses' of spelling in Present-day English.
2) Identify the sound changes that Hart describes in this extract from his book.

2 Major Phonological Changes

2.1 The Great Vowel Shift

One systematic phonological change is particularly responsible for the mismatch of spelling and pronunciation today. This is the Great Vowel Shift (abbreviated GVS), which started around the 15th century and reached completion in the late 16th or early 17th century. In this, each long vowel changed its sound quality, but the distinction between one vowel and the next was maintained. The five Middle English long vowels [a:], [ɛ:], [e:], [ɔ:], and [o:] were raised, and the vowels [i:] and [u:], which could not be raised any further, became diphthongized. First they developed the intermediate forms [əi] and [əu] respectively; then they changed further into [aɪ] and [aʊ].

Fig. 11: The Great Vowel Shift

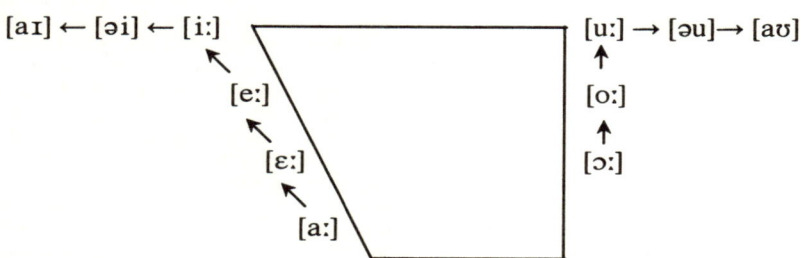

Why and how did this dramatic shift occur, which was to change the whole phonological system of the language? It is generally assumed that these series of changes were connected, with a move in one vowel causing a move in another. It could have been that the shift started from the raising of the mid vowels [e:] and [o:], which "pushed" the higher vowels upwards in a chain reaction (a so-called *push-chain* reaction), leaving a space into which the lower vowels were "dragged" (causing a so-called *drag-chain* reaction).[3] The question why the Great Vowel Shift happened is even more difficult to answer. There may have been sociolinguistic reasons for this, with the middle and upper classes trying to distinguish themselves from the lower classes by changing their pronunciation.[4]

Tab. 25: Sound Changes From Middle English to Present-day English

ME	EModE	PdE	example
[a:]	[ɛ:]	[eɪ]	*name*
[ɛ:]	[e:]	[i:]	*sea*
[e:]	[i:]	[i:]	*see*
[i:]	[əi]	[aɪ]	*ride*
[ɔ:]	[o:]	[əʊ]	*boat*
[o:]	[u:]	[u:]	*boot*
[u:]	[əu]	[aʊ]	*cloud*

From the late 16th or early 17th century to the 18th century, i.e. in the Late Modern English period, some of the vowels which had been affected by the Great Vowel Shift developed even further. Early Modern English [e:] was raised to [i:], so that words like *sea* and *see* became homophones (with the exceptions of *break, great,* and *steak*). Furthermore, Early Modern English [ɛ:] and [o:] became diphthongized into [eɪ] and [ou] respectively. In British English, [ou] developed further into [əu], but was retained in American English. For a survey of the sound changes of long vowels from Middle English to Present-day English, see table 25 above.

2.2 Further Vowel Changes

Other changes took place that were also related to the Great Vowel Shift. The raise of [ɔ:] to [o:] had left a gap in the vowel system. A new [ɔ:] filled it, which developed from the monophthongization of Middle English [au] and the later lengthening of [ɔ] before [r] (see below). The other gap left was [a:], caused by the raise of [a:] to [ɛ:]. It was filled by an [æ:] that had developed from [a:].[5] Moreover, the long [u:] that had developed from [o:] during the Great Vowel Shift was later sometimes shortened to [ʊ] in words of one syllable, especially those ending in a single consonant (*good*, *took*, *hood*). If the shortening had taken place early, this [ʊ] then took part in the general change of [ʊ] to [ʌ], as is the case in *blood*, *flood*, *glove*, and *done*.

These and further major vowel changes are summarized in the tables 26–28 below and examples are given. Note that new homophones developed.

Tab. 26: Early Modern English Diphthongs

ME	EModE	LModE/PdE	examples
[au]	[ɒ:]	[ɔ:]	*cause, law*
[aɪ]	[ɛ:]	[eɪ]	*maid, day*
[ɪu]	[ju:] / [u:]		*new, rude*
[ɔu]	[ɔ:] > [o:]	[əu] (British English)	*soul, know*

Tab. 27: Further Developments of Early Modern English Long Vowels

ME	EModE	LModE/PdE	examples
[ɛ:]	[ɛ]		*breath*
[o:]	[u:], early > [ʊ]	[ʌ]	*blood, flood*
[o:]	[u:], later > [ʊ]		*book, foot*

To recall these numerous developments may seem difficult, but in fact the spelling of Present-day English often reveals how the sounds were spoken in Middle English and Early Modern English. Table 29 helps you to infer Middle English pronunciation from Present-day English spelling, including the types of sound changes that happened from the 15th century onwards. For instance, *sweet* was pronounced [swe:t] in Middle English, *sun* [sʊn] and *taught* [tauxt].

Tab. 28: Short Vowels

ME	EModE	LModE	examples
[a]	[æ]	[æ:] when preceding voiceless fricatives and [n] + [s] or [t] > British English [ɑ:]	*half, fast, answer*
[ʊ]	[ʊ]	[ʌ]	*but*
[-ə(n)]	∅		*meet, met*

Tab. 29: Infering Middle English Pronunciation from Present-day English Spelling

PdE		examples	ME	sound changes
/iː/	⟨ee⟩	*sweet*	[eː]	GVS [eː] > [iː]
	⟨ea⟩	*clean,*	[ɛː]	GVS [ɛː] > [eː] > LModE > [iː]
	⟨ie⟩	*niece*	[eː]	OF [ie], ON [eː], GVS [eː] > [iː]
/ɪ/	⟨i⟩	*ship*	[ɪ]	-
/e/	⟨e⟩	*bed*	[ɛ]	-
/æ/	⟨a⟩	*that*	[a]	EModE [a] > [æ]
/ʌ/	⟨u/o⟩	*sun, love*	[ʊ]	> [ʌ]
	⟨ou⟩	*cousin,*		OF [u], [o] or [y]
	⟨o/u⟩	*money, just*		
/ɑː/	⟨a⟩	*charm*	[ar]	18th c.: lengthening of the vowel and loss of postvocalic [r]
		ask, staff	[a]	> EModE [æ] + voiceless spirants or nasal + [s] or [t] > [æː] > [ɑː]
	⟨au⟩	*aunt*	[aʊ]	OF [ã]
/ɒ/	⟨o⟩	*dog, soft*	[ɔ]	> [ɒ]
	⟨a⟩	*was, watch*	[a]	17th c. > [ɒ] when preceded by [w]
/ɔː/	⟨au⟩	*taught,*	[aʊ],	+ [x, v, 1 , w, ɣ]
	⟨a⟩	*talk*	[a]	
	⟨aw⟩	*hawk, thaw,*	[aʊ]	
	⟨ou⟩	*law*		
	⟨au⟩	*bought*	[ɔʊ]	+ [x]
		sauce	[aʊ]	OF [au]
/ʊ/	⟨u⟩	*put*	[ʊ]	[ʊ]
	⟨oo⟩	*good, foot*	[oː]	GVS [oː] > [uː], > [ʊ]
/uː/	⟨oo⟩	*food, moon*	[oː]	GVS [oː] > [uː]
	⟨ou⟩	*route, soup*	[uː]	French loans after ~1400
/juː/		*Tuesday, new*	[ɪʊ]	OE [iː] + [w], > [ɪʊ]
		knew	[ɛʊ]	OE [eo] + [w], > [ɛʊ]
		few	[ɛʊ]	OE [æɑ] or [æː] + [w] > EModE [ɛʊ]

PdE	examples	ME	sound changes
/ɜ:/	*serve, shirt* *birch, her* *turn, world*	[ε + r] [ɪ + r]/ [ʊ + r]	18th c.: loss of [r]
/ə/	*about, bishop*	[ə]	any unaccented vowel or diphthong
/eɪ/	*name* *day, way* *break, great*	[a:] [εɪ] [ε:]	GVS [a:] > [ε:] > [eɪ] [εɪ] > [ε:] > [eɪ] exception: GVS [ε:] > [eɪ]
/aɪ/	*time, child*	[i:]	GVS [i:] > [aɪ]
/ɔɪ/	*choice, noise*	[ɔɪ]	from Old French
/əʊ/	*home* *soul, own, blow*	[ɔ:] [ɔʊ]	GVS [ɔ:] > [o:] > [oʊ] > [əʊ] OE [a:], [o:] + [w] or [ɣ]
/aʊ/	*house, ground, fowl*	[u:]	GVS [u:] > [aʊ]
/ɪə/	*here* *ear*	[e: + r] [ε: + r]	18th century: vocalization of post-vocalic [r]
/eə/	*care* *hair, their* *bear, there*	[a: + r] [εɪ + r] [ε: + r]	vocalization of post-vocalic [r]
/ʊə/	*poor, boor* *sure, pure*	[o:, ɔ: + r] [ɪʊ, εʊ+r]	vocalization of post-vocalic [r]

2.3 Consonants

Like most of the short vowels, the consonants of English have been fairly stable. Within the Modern English period, certain losses occurred:

a) At the beginning of the Modern English period, the long consonants were given up.[6]

b) From the 14th to the 16th centuries, final [b] and [g] disappeared after nasals (*thumb, long*).

c) From the 15th century onwards, [h] was no longer spoken before [w] (*what, when*).

d) The voiceless palatal fricative [ç] was no longer spoken in words like *bright* and *sigh* (apart from some Scottish dialects).

e) The corresponding voiceless velar fricative [x] was either no longer spoken, as in *taught* and *bough*, or became [f], as in *enough* and *laugh* (apart from some Scottish dialects).

f) In the 17th century, [k] and [g] disappeared before [n] (*knee, gnaw*).

g) The lateral [1] was no longer spoken in words like *talk* and *half*.

h) The sound [w] was no longer spoken in words like *sword, answer, write*, and others.

i) From the 18th century onwards, [r] was vocalized after vowels and in final position (in RP).

Tab. 30: Consonantal Changes

	ME	from EModE until now	examples
"losses"	[tt], [dd]	simplification of long consonants	*sit, bid, dwell*
	[b], [g]	after nasals	*limb, sing*
	[h]	before [w]	*where, which*
	[ç]	Ø	*knight, right*
	[x]	Ø or > [f]	*daughter, rough*
	[k], [g]	before [n]	*kneel, gnash*
	[1]	before [k], [f], [v], [m] in monosyllabic words, also in *should*	*stalk, calf, calves,palm*
	[w]	before some back rounded vowels, at the beginning of unstressed syllables, before [r]	*sword, answer, write*
	post-vocalic [r]	vocalization to [ə] > a) lengthening of preceding vowel b) [ɛ] / [ɪ] / [ʊ] + [ə] > [ɜː] c) centering diphthongs: [eː] / [ɛː] / [oː] + [ə] > [ɪə] / [eə] / [ʊə] (or [ɔː])	*arm, horse* *herb, birth, curse* *here, pear, poor*
"gains"	[ŋg]	> [ŋ]	*sing, coming, song*
	[-zj-]	> [ʒ] + word-finally in French loans	*vision, treasure* *beige*
	[-r]	[ɪə], [eə], [ʊə], see above	
	Ø	[h] word-initially in French loans	*habit, heritage*

Some of the losses gave rise to new phonemes. The deletion of final [g] allowed [ŋ] to stand in contrast to other nasals (*sing* vs. *sin*), and as a consequence, the new phoneme /ŋ/ emerged, which had previously been an allophone of /n/ preceding velars. The vocalization of post-vocalic [r] resulted in the new Present-day English diphthongal phonemes /ɪə, eə, ʊə/ and the vowel phoneme /ɜː/ – and also in the introduction of [ɑː] and [ɔː] into words like *cart* and *port*.

The consonantal phoneme /ʒ/ derives from a coalescence of [z] + [j]. In the 17th century, the cluster [zj] started to become palatalized, leading to the new phoneme. Subsequently, /ʒ/ also appeared in French loanwords, like *rouge*, *beige*, and *prestige*. Moreover, /h/ was initially added to British English through French loans like *habit*, *herb*, and *humble*, where no [h] sound was pronounced originally in Vulgar Latin and Romance (spelling pronunciation).

ⱦ ⱦ Exercise 23: Phonological History

Trace the phonological history of these Old English words by transcribing their Old English, Middle English, and Present-day English pronunciation.

1)	*tīma*	'time'	10)	*sǣ*	'sea'	19)	*fæst*	'fast'
2)	*ynce*	'inch'	11)	*hēap*	'heap'	20)	*hlūd*	'loud'
3)	*seofon*	'seven'	12)	*fūl*	'foul'	21)	*lǣfan*	'leave'
4)	*crabba*	'crab'	13)	*fōda*	'food'	22)	*sāpe*	'soap'
5)	*hnutu*	'nut'	14)	*hām*	'home'	23)	*standan*	'stand'
6)	*hȳdan*	'hide'	15)	*iung*	'young'	24)	*sunne*	'sun'
7)	*cēse*	'cheese'	16)	*cnēo*	'knee'	25)	*tēþ*	'teeth'
8)	*hwēol*	'wheel'	17)	*cyssan*	'kiss'	26)	*dæg*	'day'
9)	*dǣd*	'deed'	18)	*ēast*	'east'			

ⱦ Exercise 24: The Great Vowel Shift

1) Show the changes effected by the GVS by transcribing the following words phonetically both in Middle English and in Present-day English: *mice*, *mouse*, *geese*, *goose*, *break*, *broke*, and *name*.

2) The following are phonetic transcriptions of Middle English words. Write their present-day developments in phonetic transcription and in normal orthography.

1) [bɔːst]	5) [guːn]	9) ['hiːdən]	13) [poːl]	17) [uːt]
2) [broːd]	6) [juː]	10) ['meːtən]	14) [pɔːl]	18) [wiːd]
3) ['daːmə]	7) [kaːs]	11) [miːn]	15) [rɛːd]	
4) [grɛːt]	8) [liːs]	12) [paːs]	16) [saːf]	

ⱦ ⱦ Exercise 25: Vowels: from Middle English to Present-day English[7]

1) The following words contained the vowel [a] in Middle English:

A *lap, at, add, back, bag; staff, craft, path, glass*
B *ash, crash, flash; all, call, hall, tall*
C *calf, half, halves; alms, calm, psalm*
D *halt, bald, salt; chalk, walk*

Which vowel has developed from Middle English [a]

a) before a voiceless fricative (except [ʃ])?
b) before a stop?
c) before final [1] or [1] plus an alveolar stop?
d) before [1] plus [k] (what happened to the [1])?
e) before [1] plus a labiodental fricative (what happened to the [1])?
f) before [1] plus a nasal (what happened to the [1])?
g) How do typical British and American usages differ in their developments of [a] in these words?

2) The following words contained the vowel [ɔ] in Middle English:

A *hop, pot, odd, dock*
B *dog, frog, log*
C *soft, off, lost, cross, cloth*
D *roll, folk, yolk*

Which vowel has developed from Middle English [ɔ]

a) before a voiced velar stop?
b) before most stops?
c) before [1]?
d) before a voiceless fricative?
e) How do typical British and American usages differ in their developments of this vowel?

3) The following words had [ʊ] in Middle English:

A *bud, buck, puff, skull, blush, rush, hush, cut, nut, but*
B *bull, full, pull, push, put*

a) What is the usual development of Middle English [ʊ]?
b) In what environment did it remain unchanged?
c) Which of the words above is an exception to the generalization in b)?

4) The following words contained the vowel [ɛ:] in Middle English:

A *steak, great, break, yea*
B *sweat, threat, head, bread, death, breath*
C *clean, cream, heath, leaf, mead, meat*

a) In the second group of words the long vowel was shortened to [ɛ] / [e]. Before what kind of consonants did the shortening occur?
b) Which sound in Present-day English usually corresponds to Middle English [ɛ:]?

3 Grammar

Morphological and syntactic developments in Early Modern English continued the trend established during Middle English times that changed the English grammar from a synthetic to an analytic system. Compared to Present-day English, however, alternative forms or constructions still co-existed, sometimes even in the same piece of writing. Examples are the forms of verbal inflection, personal pronouns, the comparative and superlative of adjectives, and the optional use of the operator *do*. Eventually, certain forms gained ground at the expense of others, and by the end of the 17th century, most of the various developments were completed. Subsequently, two innovations should be mentioned, which occurred within the verbal system: the increasing use of the perfect and the progressive. Both are often subsumed under the term *aspect*, which refers to the duration of the activity indicated by the verb.

3.1 Nouns

The only inflectional endings left were the genitive singular and the plural, which are still used today. Nevertheless, some old plural forms could be found occasionally. A handful of them resisted the principle of analogy and have survived to the present.

3.2 Pronouns

The Early Modern English pronoun system underwent several alterations, which led to the pronominal system as it is used nowadays. Three changes in particular were responsible for the establishment of the present-day system of personal pronouns:

a) the disuse of *thou*, *thy*, and *thee*
   In the 13th century, the singular forms *thou*, *thy*, and *thee* came to be used in intimate and informal situations, while the plurals *ye* and *you* developed into polite and respectful forms of address. This development mirrors the use of *tu* and *vous* in French, and *Du* and *Sie* in German. In the course of time, the singular forms disappeared altogether.[8]

b) the substitution of *you* for *ye*
   In the 14th century, the objective *you* began to replace the nominative *ye*; and *ye* finally became obsolete in the late 17th century.

c) the new pronoun *its*
   In the later part of the 16th century, the possessive neuter *its* arose, superseding Middle English *his*. The older nominative and objective *hit* had already lost its *h*- when unstressed, and eventually the *h*-less form came to be used in stressed positions as well. Nevertheless, *his* remained the proper form of the possessive

until the late 17th century and still occurred in contexts in which we would nowadays use *its*.

Tab. 31: The Personal Pronouns in Early Modern English

Nominative	*I*	*thou*	*he*	*(h)it*	*she*
Objective	*me*	*thee*	*him*	*(h)it*	*her*
Possessive	*my/mine*	*thy/thine*	*his*	*his, it, its*	*her/hers*
Nominative	*we*	*ye/you*	*they*		
Objective	*us*	*you/ye*	*them / (h)em*		
Possessive	*our/ours*	*your/yours*	*their / theirs*		

In addition to these changes within the system of personal pronouns, the originally interrogative pronoun *who* (Old English *hwā*) became more and more used as a relative pronoun. In Middle English, the almost universal relative pronoun was *that*, which was later joined by the originally interrogative *which*. From the 16th century onwards, *who* also started to occur as a relative pronoun, mainly with reference to persons. In the course of the 17th century, *that* was increasingly restricted to defining clauses, while the relatives *who* and *which* became confined to personal and non-personal nouns respectively. Eventually, the pronouns became used as they are today.

3.3 Adjectives

The adjective had already become invariable but the use of the comparative and superlative forms were not as regularized as they are nowadays. There was more variation in the use of *-er* and *-est* on the one hand and *more* and *most* on the other. Furthermore, a double comparative or superlative was possible (*more larger, most highest*).

3.4 Verbs

The strong verbs continued either to become weak, or to be lost altogether. The Present-day English irregular forms of verbs may have been weak (*think, thought, thought*) or strong (*sing, sang, sung*) in former times. In those strong verbs that survived, the Old English four principal parts (infinitive, past tense singular, past tense plural, past participle) were reduced to three, and the new past tense form was sometimes derived from the old singular and sometimes from the old plural form.

The personal endings were somewhat simplified from those of Middle English. The ending of the third person singular present varied according to region: the north used *-es*, while the south favored *-eth*. During the 16th century, the northern form expanded to the south, and finally took over. By the end of the century it had become the common ending in all parts of the country.

Tab. 32: Personal Endings in Early Modern English

personal pronoun(s)	present tense	past tense
I	*fall*	*fell*
thou	*fallest, fallst*	*fell, fellest, fellst*
he, she	*falleth, falls*	*fell*
we, you, they	*fall*	*fell*

Furthermore the increasing use of the operator *do* and contractions such as *don't* and *won't* are worth mentioning. Contrary to modern usage, the subjunctive was still being used widely, and *shall* occurred with all persons.

Two remarkable developments occurred after the Early Modern English period, namely the increased use of the perfect and the progressive. The foundation for the emergence of these constructions had already been laid in the Middle English period, but they have been common only since the 18th century. The perfective aspect probably originates from an Old English construction which consisted of an auxiliary and a past participle functioning as an adjective. It was formed by one of the auxiliaries *habban* and *wesan* and the past participle of the verb (compare Old English *Hæfde se gōda Gēata lēoda cempan gecorene*).[9] In Middle English, the perfect was only used for stylistic reasons, especially for emphasis and metrical purposes; moreover the present perfect and past tenses were interchangeable. There were two auxiliaries that could be used, depending on the syntactic properties of the verb. Intransitive verbs formed their perfect with *be*, and transitive verbs with *have* (compare German *ich bin gelaufen* with *ich habe dich besucht*). This is still the case in Early Modern English, but in the course of the last two centuries, *have* eventually became used for the perfective aspect and *be* for the passive and progressive only. Forms with *be* have survived in some fixed expressions, such as *it is gone, it is done*. The functional difference between the perfect and the past tenses finally developed in Late Modern English times.

The ending of the progressive developed from Middle English *-ing*, which was originally from the old verbal noun ending *-ung* (compare German *-ung*). Old English had a corresponding construction with a present participle as predicate adjective (OE *hē wæs lǣrende* = 'he was teaching'), but this form became rare in Middle English. It seems likely that a prepositional phrase with a verbal noun led to the development of the progressive form. For example, the clause *he is on huntinge* changed into *he is a-hunting* and finally into *he is hunting*. The new form was optional until the 18th century. At the end of the 18th century, the progressive also became common in the passive voice. It is remarkable that the progressive has expanded well into the 21st century, especially forms with *be* (*he was being silly*) and *have* (*she is having coffee*), and those marking future time (*I'll be seeing you next week*).

Since the progressive and perfective forms are complex structures, consisting of an auxiliary and a non-finite verb form, the use of non-finite forms has increased considerably over the last two centuries. Moreover other non-finite constructions are being used more and more, such as the infinitive, especially the construction infinitive + accusative, the participle, and the gerund.[10]

≤ Exercise 26: Early Modern English Pronouns[11]

Consider the following passages from Shakespeare. What does the choice between the *y*-forms and *th*-forms of the second person pronoun imply?

1) [Miranda questions her father about the storm.]

Miranda	If by *your* art, my dearest father, *you* have
	Put the wild waters in this roare, allay them.
	[...]
Prospero	No harm: I have done nothing but in care of *thee*,
	(Of *thee*, my dear one, *thee*, my daughter), who
	Art ignorant of what *thou* art, nought knowing
	Of whence I am, nor that I am more better
	Than Prospero, master of a full poor cell,
	And *thy* no greater father.
	(*The Tempest, I.ii, 1-20*)

2) [King Henry doubts his son's loyalty.]

King	But wherefore do I tell these news to *thee?*
	Why, Harry, do I tell *thee* of my foes,
	Which art my nearest and dearest enemy?
	Thou that art like enough, through vassal fear,
	Base inclination, and the start of spleen,
	To fight against me under Percy's pay,
	To dog his heels, and curtsy at his frowns,
	To show how much *thou* art degenerate.
Prince	Do not think so; *you* shall not find it so;
	And God forgive them that so much have sway'd
	Your Maiesty's good thoughts away from me!
	I will redeem all this on Percy's head,
	And in the closing of some glorious day,
	Be bold to tell *you*, that I am *your* son [...]
	(*The First Part of Henry the Fourth, III.ii, 121-134*)

3) [King Claudius and Queen Gertrude urge Hamlet to cheer up.]

King	How is it that the clouds still hang on *you?*
Hamlet	Not so, my lord, I am too much in the sun
Queen	Good Hamlet, cast *thy* knighted color off,
	And let *thine* eye look like a friend on Denmark.
	Do not for ever with *thy* vailed lids
	Seek for *thy* noble father in the dust.
	Thou know'st 'tis common, all that lives must die,
	Passing through nature, to eternity.
	[...]
King	'Tis sweet and commendable in *your* nature, Hamlet,
	To give these mourning duties to *your* father;
	But *you* must know, *your* father lost a father;
	(*The Tragedy of Hamlet, Prince of Denmark, I.ii, 66- 89*)

🖎🖎 Exercise 27: Prepositions[12]

Read these lines by Shakespeare and then write the preposition that would now be used instead of the italicized preposition.

1) He came *of* an errand to mee, from Parson Hugh. (*The Merry Wives of Windsor*)
2) Therefore prepare your selfe *to* death. (*Measure for Measure*)
3) And be not iealous *on* me, gentle Brutus. (*Julius Ceasar*)
4) How? The Duke in Counsell? *In* this time of the night? (*Othello*)
5) I haue no power *upon* you; Hers you are. (*Antony and Cleopatra*)
6) Wee'l deliuer you *of* your great danger. (*Coriolanus*)
7) What thinke you *on*'t? (*Hamlet*)
8) That he which hath no stomack *to* this fight, Let him depart. (*Henry V*)
9) Meet me in the palace wood, a mile *without* the Towne. (*A Midsummer Night's Dream*)
10) *Grumio*: ... wee came downe a fowle hill, my Master riding behinde my Mistris. *Curtis*: Both *of* one horse? (*The Taming of the Shrew*)

4 Vocabulary

4.1 Early Modern English Sources of New Words

The renewed interest in the classical languages and literatures, and the rapidly developing fields of science, medicine, and the arts, made many new expressions necessary that had not yet been part of the English vocabulary. The need to write and talk about the new ideas, inventions and techniques, and the wish to enrich and improve the language, led to an immense growth of the English word stock. It is believed that about 10,000 words entered the English language during that time, though only about half of them have survived until today.[13] The largest number of borrowings originated from Latin and were mainly absorbed into the fields of biology, technology, medicine, law, theology, and the liberal arts. Most of the words came into English by way of the written language, and they were typically learned expressions. Today many of them tend to be used in the more formal styles of mostly written English.

Tab. 33: Borrowings of Early Modern English

language	examples
Latin	*accomodation, appropriate, area, capsule, complex, conspicuous, expectation, imitate, nervous, obscene, submerge*
French	*ballet, champagne, colonel, dessert, genteel, invalid, machine, naïve, scene, trophy, vase*
Greek	*anonymous, catastrophe, enthusiasm, lexicon, thermometer*
Italian	*balcony, bulletin, grotto, opera, piazza, volcano*
Spanish or Portuguese	*apricot, buffalo, cannibal, canoe, flamingo, hurricane, molasses, mosquito, tabacco*
Dutch	*brandy, easel, knapsack, landscape, yacht*

The idea of adopting words from other languages did not always meet with common consent. Some words that had been borrowed were so strange that many Englishmen disapproved of them. These pompous words were called *inkhorn terms*, and were frequently ridiculed.[14] Examples are *furibund* ('furious'), *lubrical* ('smooth, slippery, wanton'), and *turgidous* ('swollen, puffed up'). However, despite these complaints, quite a number of them were accepted into the English language, for example *ingenious, mundane, extoll, confidence*, and *contemplate*.[15]

The next largest source of borrowings was French, including military and scientific terms but also many words from the general vocabulary. Some words were also borrowed from Greek, Italian, Spanish, Portuguese, and Dutch, but their number is much smaller than the number of Latin and French borrowings. They include words to do with warfare, seafaring, commerce (including food and drinks), plants and animals, and the arts. Italian, Spanish, and Portuguese words were also often adopted in a French form, while Greek words were introduced via Latin (for examples of borrowings in Early Modern English, see table 33 above).

However, it was not only borrowings that met the need for new words. Poets rather preferred the reintroduction of native words that had become rare or obsolete, especially words that they knew from reading Chaucer, which is why these words are sometimes called *Chaucerisms*. The chief proponent of the revival of archaisms was the poet Edmund Spenser (1552-1599), but among his opponents was another famous poet, Ben Jonson (1573-1637), who considered many Chaucerisms rustic and odd. Examples are *askew*, *astound*, *blatant*, *chirrup*, *doom*, *freak*, *squall* ('to cry'), and *wrizzled* ('wrinkled, shriveled').[16] It is quite surprising that many of these words have passed from the language of poetry into common use, having since been fully accepted.

4.2 Effects of Borrowing

The effects of borrowing were far-reaching and can still be perceived today. The majority of English people considered the Latinate borrowings difficult to learn and to remember, and a number of dictionaries of so-called *hard words* were published to help them understand these words.[17] The dictionaries contained borrowings from Latin, French, Greek, and other languages, and they looked similar to our dictionaries of foreign words today. The problem with hard words was that they entered the English language in isolation. They were not "supported" by compounds, derivatives or words from other word classes of the same stem. This phenomenon has been called *dissociation*.[18] For instance, the English words *oral* and *mouth* do not belong to the same etymological family and are thus dissociated, while German *Mund* and *mündlich* are associated. Latinate words were often borrowed without their base word, because the corresponding Anglo-Saxon word expressed a common concept and was already an integral part of the English language. Thus the Latin adjective *ōrālis* was borrowed but not its corresponding noun *ōs*.

Since the Latinate words were so difficult to understand, they were often misused. Similarly sounding words could be easily confused. Examples are *epithet / epitaph*, *oracular / vernacular*, and *illiterate / illegitimate*. This misuse is called *malapropism*, after Mrs. Malaprop in Sheridan's drama *The Rivals* (1775), who confused difficult foreign words to the great delight of the audience. Now and then the misuse of these words led to a change in meaning so that some of the Latin words in English differ in meaning from the corresponding ones in other languages – and might become 'false friends' to the learner. For instance, *sensible* means 'rational' and not 'empathetic', *familiar* 'well-known' and not 'informal', *emergency* not 'the act of emerging' but 'unexpected and dangerous situation'.

In other cases, the unintelligible words were reanalyzed and reshaped on the basis of known morphemes and thus became *folk etymologies*.[19] Examples are *sparrowgrass* from *asparagus*, *cockroach* from Spanish *cucaracha*, and *mushroom* from French *mousséron*, *sirloin* from *sur loin*, *crayfish* from *écrevisse*, *causeway* from *chaussée*, *beakiron* from *bi-corne*, *cowcumber* from *cucumber* (17th century).

Another more serious effect was the impact of hard words on the remaining vocabulary. Since these words were difficult to learn and remember, many of the English avoided using them and fell back upon simple and well-known terms. In addition, the large number of synonyms, with their subtle differences in meaning, made the choice of a word even more difficult. As a consequence, nowadays relatively few words are used very regularly in everyday speech, and the richness of vocabulary in the English language due to the many borrowings mainly shows in other, mostly written styles of English.

Furthermore the overuse of the everyday words resulted in their diversity of meaning (*polysemy*) and their use in fixed phrases or idioms. This is, for instance, the case with the word *take*. It can mean 'to carry' (*take my bag*), 'to reach and hold' (*take a rope*), 'to remove' (*take books off the table*), 'to capture' (*take the town*), 'to choose / buy' (*take the grey jacket*), 'to eat / drink' (*take sugar*) etc.[20] Additionally, it occurs in idioms like *take it that* ('suppose'), *take after somebody* ('look like your mother or father'), *take off* ('leave the ground and begin to fly') etc. The verb *take* is an extreme case, but there are many other words with multiple meanings in the English language. Though the learner may initially think that English is a simple language because there are not too many words and inflections to be learned, they might change their minds when confronted with the various shades of meaning of a word and the idioms that go with it.

4.3 Later Borrowings

The expansion of the British empire in the 17th and 18th centuries led to an increase of new borrowings into the English language, which reflect the new experiences, activities, inventions and products of that time. Some of the words were brought in by the settlers, and some of them originate from the indigenous languages of the various countries. They became common in certain areas and thus contributed to the rise of the standard national varieties of English. Furthermore, due to the immense and continuing growth of science and technology, Latin has again become the source of many borrowings, compounds and derivatives. Today the manifold of international relations, global trade, transport, and tourism are also giving rise to new words.

Tab. 34: Vocabulary Borrowings from the 18th Century Onwards[21]

18th – 19th c.	language	examples
	Latin	*accumulator, auditorium, bacillus, cortex, formula, genus, habitat, hibernate, inertia, insomnia, nucleus*
	French	*amateur, brochure, boulevard, bureau, chauffeur, chiffon, garage, picnic, rouge, souvenir*
	Spanish or Portuguese (also via the Americans)	*albino, bolero, cantina, canyon, commando, lasso, merino, ranch, rodeo, samba, verandah*
	Native American	*hickory, moose, raccoon, skunk*

18th – 19th c.	language	examples
	Italian	*casino, diva, finale, inferno, mafia,* *risotto, spaghetti, studio*
	German	*kindergarten, kirsch, leitmotiv, noodle,* *quartz, rucksack, zeitgeist, waltz*
	Russian	*balalaika, parka, troika, vodka*
	Indian (Urdu and Hindi)	*chutney, jungle, karma, khaki, loot,* *purdah, pyjamas, sitar, thug, yoga*
20th c.	national varieties:	
	American English	*truck, gas, mail, diaper*
	Australian English	*robin, kangaroo, swag*
	South African English	*apartheid, tsetse, mamba*
	Nigerian English	*head-tie, akara balls*
	East African (via Kiswahili)	*safari, bwana*
	Caribbean English	*nyam, juk, door-mouth*
	Canadian English	*Digby chicken, mukluk, salt-chuck*
	languages other than English:	
	French	*cache, camouflage, déjà vu, fromage* *frais, limousine, mousse, nouvelle* *cuisine*
	Italian	*ciao, dolce vita, galleria, mascarpone,* *paparazzo, pizza, radicchio*
	Spanish	*gazpacho, basuco, macho, nacho,* *jojoba*
	Japanese	*bonsai, karate, origami, shiatsu, sushi,* *karaoke*
	Chinese	*dim sum, mah jong, tai chi, yin, yang,* *wok*
	Arabic	*islam, jihad*
	Russian	*agitprop, babushka, glasnost, gulag,* *perestroika, sputnik*

It seems that the English disposition to borrow words from other languages facilitates further growth of the English vocabulary. A summary of borrowings from the 18th century onwards is given above.

5 Text Samples

✍ ✍ Exercise 28: Margery Kempe

Margery Kempe (c.1373-c.1439) was a woman from Norfolk, who gave up married life to devote herself to religion. She made many pilgrimages and later dictated a book describing her visions, temptations, and journeys. Consider the following extract from her book (~1420).[22] (She refers to herself as 'this creature')

On a nygth, as þis creatur lay in hir bedde wyth hir husbond, sche herd a sownd of melodye so swet & delectable, hir þowt, as sche had ben in Paradyse. And þerwyth sche styrt owt of hir bedde & seyd, "Alas, þat euyr I dede synne, it is ful mery in Hevyn". Thys melody was so swete þat it passyd alle þe melodye þat euyr mygth be herd in þis world wyth-owtyn ony comparyson, & caused þis creatur whan sche herd ony myrth or melodye aftyrward for to haue ful plentyuows & habundawnt teerys of hy deuocyon wyth greet sobbyngys & syhyngys aftyr þe blysse of Heuen, not dredyng þe schamys & þe spytys of þe wretchyd world.

Present-day English Translation:

"On a night as this creature lay in her bed with her husband she heard a sound of a melody so sweet and delectable to her; she thought she were in Paradise. And so she started out of her bed and said: 'Alas that ever I did sin, it is full merry in heaven.' This melody was so sweet that it passed all the melody that ever might be heard in this world without any comparison, and caused this creature when she heard any mirth or melody afterward for to have full plenteous and abundant tears of high devotion with great sobbings and sighings after the bliss of heaven, not dreading the shames and the spites of the wretched world."

Describe differences and similarities between this early fifteenth century text in the East Midland dialect and Present-day English usage with respect to:

1) inflections of nouns
2) forms of personal and demonstrative pronouns
3) definite and indefinite articles
4) prepositions
5) strong and weak verb forms
6) development of the verb phrase
7) word order
8) spelling

✍ Exercise 29: King James Bible and the New English Bible

Under the reign of King James, a panel of over 50 university scholars translated the Bible. Their translation took several years and was published in 1611. It became known as the King James Bible and was read in churches throughout the kingdom, thus having a far-reaching influence on the population and on the language. Although the King James Bible was revised in England and America in the following centuries, its authority in the churches remained unchallenged until the publication of the New English Bible in 1970. The following texts are from the Old Testament, Exodus 14.21-25.

Early Modern English: King James Bible (1611)
And Moses stretched out his hand ouer the Sea, and the Lord caused the Sea to goe backe by a strong East winde all that night, and made the Sea dry land, and the waters were diuided. And the children of Israel went into the midst of the Sea vpon the dry ground, and the waters were a wall vnto them on their right hand, and on their left. And the Egyptians pursued, and went in after them, to the midst of the Sea, euen all Pharaohs horses, his charets and his horsemen. And it came to passe, that in the morning watch the Lord looked vnto the hoste of the Egyptians, through the pillar of fire, and of the cloude, and troubled the hoste of the Egyptians. And tooke off their charet wheeles, that they draue them heauily: So that the Egyptians said, Let vs flee from the face of Israel: for the Lord fighteth for them, against the Egyptians.

Present-day English: The New English Bible (1970)
Then Moses stretched out his hand over the sea, and the LORD drove the sea away all night with a strong east wind and turned the sea-bed into dry land. The waters were torn apart, and the Israelites went through the sea on the dry ground, while the waters made a wall for them to right and to left. The Egyptians went in pursuit of them far into the sea, all Pharaoh's horses, his chariots, and his cavalry. In the morning watch the LORD looked down on the Egyptian army through the pillar of fire and cloud, and he threw them into a panic. He clogged their chariot wheels and made them lumber along heavily, so that the Egyptians said, 'It is the LORD fighting for Israel against Egypt; let us flee.'

Compare the two versions of the Bible:

1) Are there any unusual modes of spelling in the King James Bible?

2) Can you tell if the different spellings of the two versions are due to sound changes, morphological changes, or simply different spelling conventions?

3) What can you say about the use of *and* in the King James Bible?

4) How is the conjunction *that* used in both texts?

5) What can you say about the use of the preposition *vnto* in the King James Bible and its equivalents in the later text?

6) What does *draue* (*King James Bible*, line 9) stand for? Which were the Old English and Middle English forms of this word?

✍✍ Exercise 30: Shakespeare's *Romeo and Juliet*

William Shakespeare is the best-known English writer. He was an actor and dramatist in London in the late 16th and early 17th century. His manifold works include comedies, tragedies, history plays, and poems.

Compared to the conservative style of the King James Bible, the language of Shakespeare is very innovative. It contains many new words that were not in use earlier. Consider the following extract from *Romeo and Juliet* (II.v, 25-45), and answer the questions below.[23]

Nurse	I am a-weary, give me leave a while. [1]
	Fie, how my bones ache! What a jaunce have I!
Juliet	I would thou hadst my bones, and I thy news.
	Nay, come, I pray thee speak, good, good nurse, speak.
Nurse	Jesu, what haste? Can you not stay a while? [5]
	Do you not see that I am out of breath?
Juliet	How art thou out of breath, when thou hast breath
	To say to me that thou art out of breath?
	The excuse that thou dost make in this delay
	Is longer than the tale thou dost excuse. [10]
	Is thy news good or bad? Answer to that;
	Say either, and I'll stay the circumstance.
	Let me be satisfied, is't good or bad?
Nurse	Well, you have made a simple choice; you
	know not how to choose a man. Romeo! no, not he. [15]
	Though his face be better than any man's, yet
	his leg excels all men's, and for a hand, and a foot and
	a body, though they be not to be walk'd on, yet they
	are past compare. He is not the flower of courtesy,
	but I'll warrant him, as gentle as a lamb. Go thy ways, [20]
	wench, serve God. What, have you din'd at home?

1) Explain the use of the second person pronouns.

2) Give a Present-day English equivalent to the phrase "you know not" (line 14f), and explain the difference between the Early Modern English and the Present-day English version.

3) Compare the use of the verb *would* (line 3) in this text with its use in Present-day English.

4) What kind of form is *dost* (line 9)? What does it mean?

5) Explain the form and the meaning of *hadst* in "thou hadst my bones" (line 3), *be* in "though his face be better" (line 16) and "though they be not to be walked on" (line 18).

6) Look up the words *aweary, (give) leave, fie, jaunce, nay, stay (awhile, the circumstance), (say) either, compare, warrant* and *wench* in the *Oxford English Dictionary*. How does their usage differ in comparison to Present-day English? Which of these words were used in the 16th century for the first time?

Notes:

[1] The dictionaries were: Samuel Johnson 1755, *A Dictionary of the English Language* and Noah Webster 1828, *The American Dictionary of the English Language*. By fixing pronunciation, grammar and spelling, Samuel Johnson intended to preserve the purity of the English language. Noah Webster was very conscious of American English as the national language of his country. His aim was to compile a dictionary that presented American English and not British English. He also published a spelling book in 1783 and a grammar in 1784. His books set the standards for modern American spelling and pronunciation.

[2] Taken from Freeborn [2]1998: 291/292.

[3] For a discussion of how of the Great Vowel Shift happened, see especially Aitchison [3]2001: 183-191.

[4] Leith, in his *Social History of English*, argues that a high variant of the vowel in *mate* was spoken in Essex and Kent. Since Kentish was a stigmatized dialect, the London middle and upper classes wanted to distinguish themselves from the lower classes. One possibility would have been that they started to use a vowel that was even higher than the one spoken in Kent, causing the rise of all the other vowels. Another possibility is that a lower-class merger of *meat* and *meet* triggered the vowel shift. See Leith 1983: 145-149.

[5] In Early Modern English, Middle English [a] changed to [æ], which was then lengthened before voiceless fricatives and a nasal preceding either [s] or [t]. In the 18th century, [æː] was lowered to [ɑː] in British English – American English kept a shorter version of [æː], usually transcribed as [æ] in these cases.

[6] In other descriptions, this change is also said to have happened in the Middle English period.

[7] Slightly adapted from Algeo [4]1993: 179/180.

[8] Exceptions to this are some regional dialects, certain religious texts, and the language of the Quakers.

[9] See *Beowulf* 205-6: 'had the good (one) chosen warriors of the people of the Geats'.

[10] For a discussion of the non-finite forms and their German equivalents, see Leisi/Mair [8]1999: 131-136.

[11] The following excerpts are taken from Evans 1974. The exercise is based on Algeo [4]1993: 209-12.

[12] This exercise is slightly adapted from Cable [2]1993: 112.

[13] Cf. Baugh/Cable [4]1993: 227.

[14] *Inkhorn* means *inkpot* in Present-day English.

[15] The examples are taken from Barber 1993: 180 and Baugh/Cable [4]1993: 214.

[16] For more examples, see Baugh/Cable [4]1993: 224-226.

[17] The first dictionary of hard words is Robert Cawdrey's *A Table Alphabeticall of Hard Words*, published in 1604. It is also the first monolingual English dictionary.

[18] For more detailed information see Leisi/Mair [8]1999: 51-59.

[19] Other terms used are *popular etymology* or *relative/secondary motivation*.

[20] *The Oxford Advanced Learner's Dictionary* ([6]2000) lists 30 meanings of the verb *take*.

[21] Based on Freeborn [2]1998: 403-406, 424-430.

[22] Taken from *The Book of Margery Kempe*, edited by Meech 1940, p. 11.

[23] Taken from *The Riverside Shakespeare*, edited by Evans 1974.

AMERICAN ENGLISH

1 Introduction

From the 17th century onwards, immigrants from England, Ireland, and Scotland as well as from other non-English speaking countries settled in North America. The first settlers found their new home on the East coast, and later immigrants gradually moved west. By the middle of the 19th century, the population already numbered more than 50 million.

Owing to the widespread movement within the country and the continuing mingling with new immigrants, regional dialectal differences are not as distinct as, for instance, in England. However, despite the relative uniformity of American English, there are three main dialectal areas to be observed which grew out of the early patterns of settlement. These are Northern, Midland, and Southern.

Fig. 12: The Main Dialect Divisions in the USA[1]

As a result of the homogeneity of the American language, there is a standard that is based on general use. The American English standard is often called *General American*, or, more broadly, North American English, or simply American English. It is associated with the accent which can nowadays be heard throughout the so-called Sunbelt (from Virginia to southern California). American English has developed from seventeenth-century British English. It has preserved old features of the language which have gone out of use in the standard speech of England. Archaic features can be found in pronunciation, grammar, and vocabulary. Examples are: [2]

Tab. 35: Archaic Features in American English

pronunciation	morphology and grammar	vocabulary
preservation of the [r] in AmE	AmE *gotten*, BrE *got*[3]	AmE *mad* 'angry'[4], BrE 'crazy'
pronunciation of all three syllables in *necessary, secretary*	AmE collective nouns + singular verb form, in BrE + plural verb form	AmE *fall*, BrE *autumn*
preservation of [æ] in *fast, path* etc.		AmE *rare*, BrE *under-done*[5]
⟨ile⟩ pronounced as [ɪl], as in *mobile, docile*		AmE *I guess* 'I think'[6]

But American English has also developed features of its own, mostly on the level of vocabulary. See the following examples for the innovative character of American English.

Tab. 36: American English and Its Innovative Character

pronunciation	spelling	grammar and morphology	vocabulary
change of pronunciation in *lieutenant* [luːˈtenənt]	new spelling conventions: *center, labor, defense, tire, medieval*	preference for regular past forms: *burned, learned*	new words: *belittle, boost, coverage, fall for, hitchhike, round trip, watergap*
loss of [j] after ⟨d, n, t, l, s⟩: *due, new, tune*		*as of* (originally AmE), *prefer... over*	development of new meanings: *creek*[7]

2 Spelling and Pronunciation

The American way of spelling goes back to Noah Webster, who introduced new spelling conventions in his dictionaries. His concern was to simplify spelling and to adjust it to pronunciation. He therefore omitted several "superfluous" or silent letters. His main modifications were:

a) the dropping of ⟨k⟩ in words like *music* and *logic* (formerly spelled *musick*, *logick*),

b) the reversal of ⟨e⟩ and ⟨r⟩ in words like *center* and *theater*,

c) the omission of ⟨u⟩ in, for example, *honor* and *flavor*,

d) the substitution of ⟨que⟩ with ⟨k⟩ or ⟨ck⟩, as in *check* and *risk*,

e) ⟨s⟩ instead of ⟨c⟩ in cases like *defense* and *pretense*,

f) no doubling of final ⟨l⟩ when adding a suffix as in *traveled*, *shriveled*, except in words stressed on their final syllables.

Tab. 37: The Major Differences between British and American English Pronunciation[8]

item	British English	General American
vowel	rounded [lɒt] [θɔ:t]	unrounded [lɑ:t] [θɑ:t]
/ r /	non-rhotic [wɜ:k] linking r (*the author-of*) intrusive r (*the law* [r] *is*)	rhotic [wɜ:rk] no linking r, no intrusive r
diphthongs	centering diphthongs [nɪə], [skweə], [kjʊə], [gəʊt]	no centering diphthongs [nɪr], [skwer], [kjʊr], [goʊt]
suffix vowels	['məʊməntri], ['hɒstaɪl]	[moʊmən'teri], ['hɑ:stl]
/ ɑ: /	[bɑ:θ], [dɑ:ns]	[bæθ], [dæns] 'flat a' before fricatives and before *n* followed by certain consonants
smoothing	[təə'klɒk], [kwaɪt] (*quiet*)	no smoothing
/ j / + / u: /	[nju:]	[nu:]
/ t /	[ʌnfə'getəbl]	t-flapping [ʌnfə'gerəbl]

3 Grammar

The grammar of the two national varieties is almost identical. However, there exist some notable differences between British English and American English constructions, e.g. American English *aside from* (British English *apart from*), *back of* (*behind*), *in school* (*at school*), *I just ate* (*I have just eaten*), *the most technically aware* (adverb + *aware* is unusual in British English), *I'll do it Sunday* (*I'll do it on Sunday*), *to be in the hospital* (*to be in hospital*). Collective nouns such as *government*, *family*, and *police* nearly always take singular agreement and singular pronoun substitution in American English. In British English, however, the plural forms are often used instead. Several of the modals are used differently in American English and British English. The auxiliaries *shall* and *shan't* are rarely used in American English. The auxiliary *would* characterizes a habitual activity in the past in American English; in British English, *used to* is chosen. Instead of *ought to*, American English uses *should*.

Some grammatical differences are about to disappear due to the influence of American English on British English. In informal British English, *got* is added in interrogative and negative clauses with *have* 'possess', e.g. *What have you got?*, *He hadn't got the answer*. This is not usual in American English; instead, the *do*-construction is used (*What do you have?*, *He didn't have the answer*), which is now also becoming usual in British English. The subjunctive is normal in *that*-clauses after words expressing command, hope, intention, wish etc. in American English. Today, it has become also quite acceptable in British English.[9]

4 Vocabulary

The vocabulary differences between British English and American English were caused by several factors:

a) the encounter with new objects and experiences,

b) cultural and technological developments,

c) contact with other languages, and

d) independent language change within both British English and American English.

Among the first new words were names for unknown plants, animals, and other objects which the settlers found in their new environment. Examples are *eggplant*, *squash*, *chipmunk*, and *raccoon*. Some of the words were derived from contact with the Indian tribes, including also *canoe*, *moccasin*, *wigwam*, and *moose*. The new mode of life is depicted in words like *log cabin*, *cornrib*, *popcorn*, *snow plow*, *bobsled*, *sleigh*, and *clapboard*. The new political system created the words *congressman*, *mass meeting*, *congressional*, and *presidential*. The immigrant languages were becoming part of the American environment and contributed to the American word stock. Examples are *cookie* (Dutch), *saloon, cent, chowder* (French), *kindergarten, pretzel* (German), *espresso, pasta* (Italian), *cafeteria, ranch, rodeo* (Spanish), and *schmaltz, shlemiel* (Yiddish).

Today there are many lists of British words alongside their American counterparts.[10] Some words have a single sense and a synonym in the other variety (e.g. *bookstore* vs. *bookshop*). Other words have a general meaning and, in addition a specific American or British meaning, for example, British English *caravan* corresponds to American English *trailer* in the sense of 'vehicle towed by a car'. The item *caravan* also means 'a group of people with vehicles or animals who are traveling together, especially through the desert' in both varieties. All in all, the vocabulary differences can be divided into four main categories:[11]

Tab. 38: Vocabulary Differences in British English and American English

	word / meaning	AmE	BrE
1) same word, different meaning	*pants*	'trousers'	'underpants'
	pavement	'road surface'	'sidewalk'
2) same word, additional meaning a) in AmE	*bathroom*	'room with toilet only'	'room also with bath or shower'
	dumb	'stupid'	'mute'
	rug	'a thick woollen carpet'	'a thick woollen wrap'[12]
b) in BrE	*smart*	'intelligent'	'well-groomed'
3) same word, difference in style, frequency of use	*perhaps*	formal[13]	all styles
	quite (*quite good*)	positive	neg. / neutral
	to fancy ('to like')	uncommon	common, inf.
4) same concept or item, different word	'a device that controls the flow of liquid from a pipe'	*faucet*	*tap*
	'a line of waiting people, cars, etc.	*line*	*queue*
	'a metal container'	*can*	*tin*

Nevertheless, many of the American coinings have also found their way into British English and other national varieties. This world-wide spread of Americanisms can be attributed to the dominant position of the U.S. in politics, economics, science, and technology. This holds for the former Americanisms *billion* ('a thousand million'), *cafeteria, egghead, electrocute, fan, filling station, teenager, radio,* and *TV.*

✍✍ Exercise 31: British and American Vocabulary[14]

Try to find the correct American English words for the items depicted in the picture below. The corresponding British English words are: *engine driver, carriage, lorry, flyover, sleeper, motorway, estate car, caravan, rowing boat, sailing boat, bathing costume, luggage, bonnet, windscreen, boot, silencer, accumulator, number plate, braces, spanner, trainers, dustbin, phone box, letter box.*

Fig. 13: Vocabulary Differences between American and British English

5 Outlook: English Today

Due to the colonial expansion of Great Britain in the 19th century and the emergence of the United States as a world power in the 20th century, English has developed into a global language. Today it is one of the languages most used in the media, international politics, as a means of communication between different ethnic groups of a nation as well as between people of different nationalities (*lingua franca*), in scientific writing, in business, and in computer technology. Although the English language answers many needs in an age of mobility, globalization, and the computer industry, it has also been criticized as a language of suppression and imperialism.[15] Nevertheless, it has reached the stage where it has become a valuable cultural and economic tool for many countries all over the world.

The spread of English can be depicted as three concentric circles.[16] The inner circle presents the countries in which English has traditionally been a first language, for instance Great Britain, the USA, and Australia. The middle circle encompasses the use of English as a second language, in countries like India, Kenya or Malaysia. Finally the outer, expanding circle includes the use of English as a foreign language, in countries where a proficiency in English is considered politically important. Examples are most of the European countries, China, and Japan. Whatever circle we are in – we can start from the assumption that a supranational single standard of English exists, at least in formal writing. To the inner circle belong several national standards, such as British and American English, Scottish, and Canadian English. Some scholars also assume that a standard English as a second language has emerged in countries such as India or Nigeria.

Despite extensive codification of English and the enormous influence of print media, the English language is still changing. We can observe changes on the phonological, morphological, lexical, and syntactic level. The most obvious changes occur on the lexical level. There is certainly a need for linguistic action when newly developed ideas or concepts have to be named, but neologisms not only serve to verbalize new thoughts and concepts, they also mark style. In this case, there is no real necessity to express new ideas verbally, but there is a psychological, stylistic need to set oneself off against existing communicative conventions. Today, the word-formation types of shortenings has become quite fashionable. Examples are JIT ('just in time'), MIPS ('million(s) (of) instructions per second'), *buppie* (black yuppie'), *sit-tragedy* ('situation tragedy'), *lens* ('contact lens'), and *edutainment* ('education + entertainment'). The trend to abbreviate also shows in phrases (or even clauses) that become attributive, compare, for instance *back-to-basics* (*movement*), *live-now-pay-later* (*set*), *nine-to-five* (*job*), and *out-of-body* (*feeling*).[17]

Morphological changes mainly concern the regularization of irregular forms, for instance plurals (e.g. *index – indexes / indices* for prices and wages) and strong verbs (e.g. *learn, learned / learnt*). Corpus-based research nowadays makes it possible to document shifting frequencies of linguistic patterns.[18] The higher the frequency of a variant and the lower the frequency of another, alternative option, the more likely it is that the more common one will achieve the status of a standard. A syntactic pattern that is apparently still gaining ground is the progressive.[19]

There is evidence of newly emerging phonetic patterns in British English. Certain forms are mainly used by younger people of the upper classes and in certain professional circles. They may indicate the direction in which RP is developing. Examples of this new pattern are /eə/ becoming monophthongal /ɛ:/ and the loss of /ɔə/ from the phoneme inventory.[20]

Despite these and other ongoing changes, it is, however, surely not the case that the world-wide intelligibility of English is at stake. Most of the changes are matters of frequency, and they will take a certain time to be assimilated. With the countries of this world still getting closer, we can assume that the spread of the English language has not yet come to an end.

Notes:

[1]   This map is taken from Crystal 1988: 225.

[2]   See Marckward/Dillard [2]1980: 69-90.

[3]   Except in the senses 'to have' and 'to be obliged to'.

[4]   Went out of use in British English but has recently been reintroduced.

[5]   For meat left slightly raw after cooking.

[6]   British English certainly has the verb *guess* in the sense 'estimate'.

[7]   'Any small stream' vs. British English 'a small arm of the sea or river'.

[8]   Based on Wells 1982: 117-127, 212-263.

[9]   See also the entries labeled 'American Usage' in *The Oxford Guide to English Usage* [2]1993.

[10] See, for instance, Crystal 1995: 309.

[11] The following examples are taken from Trudgill/Hannah [3]1994: 89-91.

[12] American English *afghan*.

[13] The word *maybe* is used instead.

[14] Slightly adapted from Cable [2]1993: 148-150.

[15] See, for instance, Pennycook 1998 or Phillipson 1992.

[16] See Kachru 1985: 12-15; further Crystal 1995: 309.

[17] For a study of recent creative neologisms and their institutionalization, see Fischer 1998.

[18] Linguistic corpora are collections of texts whose size ranges from one to a hundred million words, or even more than that. An example of an English grammar text that takes into account the frequency of usage of the various syntactic patterns is the *Longman Grammar of Spoken and Written English*.

[19] See Mair/Hundt 1995: 111-122. On the state of English see also Graddol 1997 and Kortmann 2001.

[20] See Gimson/Cruttenden [5]1994: 82-83 for further details.

APPENDIX

Solutions to the Exercises

✍ Exercise 1: The Numbers *Four* and *Five* in Various Indo-European Languages

1) E
2) A and F, B and D, C and G
3) A and F
4) G

✍✍✍ Exercise 2: Major Changes from Indo-European to Germanic

1) E cf. *magnī* vs. *micle, miclan*
2) C *b, d, g > p, t, k*
3) C *bh, dh, gh > b, d, g*
4) A IE **mater*, Grimm's Law and Verner's Law *t > θ > ð* (→ WGmc *d*)
5) B IE *ā* > Gmc *ō*
6) D

✍ Exercise 3: Insular Hand I

"The abbot Aelfric sends his friendly greetings to Sigeferth. I was told that you said about me that, in my English writings, I teach something different than your religious hermit at home. This is because he clearly says that parish priests are allowed to marry, and I contradict this in my writings."

✍✍ Exercise 4: Insular Hand II

1) "Britain island is eight hundred miles long and two hundred broad and here are on this island five languages: English and British and Welsh and Scottish and Pictish and book Latin. First were inhabitants of this land the Britons."

2) ['brɪt:ənə 'i:jlɑnd ɪs 'ɛhtɑ hʊnd 'mi:lɑ lɑŋg ɑnd twɑ: hʊnd brɑ:d ɑnd he:r sɪnd ɔn θɪs 'i:jlɑnd fi:f jə'θeodə. 'ɛŋglɪʃ ɑnd 'brɪt:ɪʃ ɑnd wɪlʃ ɑnd 'ʃʏt:ɪʃ ɑnd 'pʏçtɪʃ ɑnd bo:k 'le:dən. 'e:rəst 'we:rɔn 'bu:ənd 'θɪs:əs 'lɑndəs 'brit:əs]

3) "The British island is a hundred miles long and two hundred miles wide, and five languages are spoken here on this island. These are English, British, Welsh, Scottish, Pictish, and also written Latin. The first inhabitants of this island were the Britons. "

✍✍ Exercise 5: Phonetic Transcription

1) [ˈfʏksən]
2) [wiːf]
3) [ˈwiːvəs]
4) [bæθ]
5) [ˈbaðɪɑn]
6) [sæːs]
7) [ˈnɔzu]
8) [lyːs]
9) [ˈluːzɑ]
10) [hɑːm]
11) [hrɪŋg]
12) [ˈhlʏnzɪɑn]
13) [ˈɑːxtə]
14) [ɛˀx]
15) [ʃæɑp]
16) [ʃæᵃft]
17) [brʏdʒ]
18) [ˈdæjəs]

✍ Exercise 6: The Letters ⟨c⟩ and ⟨g⟩

1) A, D   ⟨c⟩ = [k]
   B, C   ⟨c⟩ = [tʃ]
   E, F   ⟨g⟩ = [g]
   G, I   ⟨g⟩ = [j]
   H   ⟨g⟩ = [ɣ]
2) [k] / [g]
3) [k] / [ɣ]
4) [tʃ] / [j]

✍✍ Exercise 7: Bede's *Ecclesiastical History*

1) [ˈkʏnɪŋg]
2) [ˈkɛntˌriːtʃə]
3) [ˈmɪçtɪj]
4) [ˈhævdə]
5) [jəˈmæːrʊ]
6) [ˈmɪtʃəl]
7) [ˈæᵃxtə]
8) [ˈθʏsːʊm]
9) [ˈlæːdːə]
10) [ˈdɑɣʊm]

11) [jə'wʏrtʃɑn]
12) ['spræːtʃə]
13) [hwɛltʃ]

✍ ✍ Exercise 8: Mutated Vowels

1) *bæcþ*
2) *secgan*
3) *hilpþ*
4) *gǣt*
5) *fēdan*
6) *fyllan*
7) *mǣst*
8) *fẏlþ*
9) *hīera*

✍ ✍ ✍ Exercise 9: Old English Inflections

1) A
2) E
3) G
4) B
5) C
6) D
7) B, F

✍ ✍ Exercise 10: Weak and Strong Verbs

1) Weak: A, C, D, F, I, J; Strong: B, E, G, H

2) The second verb has a causative meaning:

   fall: move downwards
   fell: to cause to fall, strike down
   lie: to be in a horizontal position
   lay: to cause to lie
   sit: to be in a position with the weight of your body on your buttocks and the
           top part of your body up right, for example, on a chair
   set: to cause to sit

3) The strong verbs gave rise to corresponding weak verbs ending in -*jan* which
   had a causative meaning. The weak verbs underwent i-mutation due to the [j] in
   –*jan* (*falljan* > *fellan*, *lagjan* > *lecgan; *satjan* > *settan*).

4) The weak verbs are those which were created after their strong counterparts: *fell – felled – felled* (from *fall – fell – fallen*), *set – set – set* (from *sit – sat – sat*), lay – *laid – laid* (from *lie – lay – lain*)

✍✍ Exercise 11: Word Order

1) Identification of the clause elements in the main clauses and the order of the subjects and verbs.

Hēr nam breohtrīc cining offan dohter ēadburge. ꞇ on his dagum cōmon ǣrest .
A V   S   O   A   V   A
iii.scipu norðmanna of hereða lande. ꞇ þā se gerēfa þǣr tō rād. ꞇ hē wolde
S   A   A   S   A   V   S   V
drīfan tō ðes ciniges tūne... ꞇ hine man ofslōh þā. Ðæt wǣron þā ērestan scipu
A   O   S   V   A   S V   S
deniscra manna þe angel cynnes land gesōhton.

2) "Here king Beorhtric married Offa's daughter Eadburh. In these days the first three ships of Northmen arrived from Hörthaland. Then the reeve rode there. He wished them to be brought to the King's manor because he did not know who they were. Then he was killed there. These were the first Danish ships that landed on English territory."

✍✍ Exercise 12: Scandinavian Borrowings

Present-day English	Old Norse	Native Old English
1) *bait* (vb.)	*beita*	*bǣtan*
2) *call* (vb.)	*kalla*	*ceallian*
3) *cast* (vb.)	*kasta*	*weorpan*
4) *get* (vb.)	*geta*	**gietan*
5) *high* (adj.)	*hár*	*hēah*
6) *loan* (sb.)	*lán*	*lǣn*
7) *loose* (adj.)	*lauss*	*lēas*
8) *race* ('rush') (sb.)	*rás*	*rǣs*
9) *raise* (vb.)	*reisa*	*rǣran*
10) *scab* (sb.)	*skabbr*	*sceabb*
11) *sister* (sb.)	*systir*	*sweoster, swuster*
12) *skirt* (sb.)	*skyrta*	*scyrte*
13) *swain* (sb.)	*sveinn*	*swān*

| 14) | *weak* (adj.) | *veikr* | *wāc* |
| 15) | *window* (sb.) | *vindauga* | *ēagþyrel* |

✍ Exercise 13: Lord's Prayer

1) The letters of the Old English writing system that have been lost from the alphabet are ⟨æ⟩, ⟨ð⟩, ⟨þ⟩, and also ⟨ƿ⟩.

2) The letter ⟨v⟩ is used at the beginning of a word (e.g. *vs*) and ⟨u⟩ is used medially (e.g. *giue*).

3) The different forms of Old English for the word *our* are *ūre*, *ūrum*, and *ūrne*. Old English has more than one form for this word as it has cases.

4) Three phrases from the Wycliffe translation in which the use of prepositions differs from that in the King James version: *thi kyngdom come to* vs. *thy kingdome come*; *yeue to us – giue vs*, *foryeue to us* vs. *forgiue vs*.

5) Three phrases from the Wycliffe translation in which the word order differs from that in the Old English version: *Fæder ūre* vs. *Oure fadir*; *sī þīn nama gehālgod* vs. *halowid be thi name*; *ne gelǣd þū ūs* vs. *lede us not*.

6) The Middle English version appears more similar to the Early Modern English version than to the Old English version due to similar word order, use of prepositions, vocabulary, relative clauses, and the position of *not*.

✍✍✍ Exercise 14: The Description of 'Scyld's Funeral Ship' from *Beowulf*

> "There at the harbor stood the ringed prow
> icy and eager to set out, the noble's vessel;
> they laid down the dear king,
> the ring distributor on the bosom of the ship,
> the mighty by the mast. There were many precious things
> from far away, treasure was loaded,
> I did not hear a ship more nobly equipped with
> war weapons and war armours,
> sword and coats of mail. On his breast lay
> a great many treasures, that should go with him
> in the possession of the flood, far away."

This is a recent free rendering by Seamus Heaney:[1]

> "A ring-whorled prow rode in the harbour,
> ice-clad, outbound, a craft for a prince.
> They stretched their beloved lord in his boat,
> laid out by the mast, amidships,
> the great ring-giver. Far-fetched treasures

were piled upon him, and precious gear.
I never heard before of a ship so well furbished
with battle-tackle, bladed weapons
and coats of mail. The massed treasure
was loaded on top of him: it would travel far
on out into the ocean's sway."

✍✍ Exercise 15: Transcription of Middle English

1) [a'lɔ:nə]	12) ['fɛɪlə]
2) ['bɛ:tən]	13) [flat]
3) ['bi:tən]	14) ['fo:də]
4) ['bla:mə]	15) ['lʊvə]
5) [blo:d]	16) [prə'se:dən]
6) ['bɔ:ðə]	17) ['rɔ:də]
7) [brɪçt]	18) [ʃo:]
8) [do:m]	19) ['stre:tə]
9) [du:n]	20) [tɔp]
10) ['du:tə]	21) [wo:d]
11) ['drɛ:dən]	22) ['je:ldən]

✍ Exercise 16: The Lengthening and Shortening of Vowels

1) aker	B	12) holden	A
2) beren	B	13) hope	B
3) bever	B	14) kinde	A
4) blosme	C	15) naddre	C
5) cold	A	16) sutherne	D
6) dore	B	17) tale	B
7) fedde	C	18) today	E
8) feeld	A	19) us	E
9) fiftene	C	20) wepenes	D
10) finden	A	21) wimmen	C
11) ground	A	22) womb	A

✍ Exercise 17: Middle English Personal Pronouns

1) And in his gentle heart he thought immediately
2) How mighty and how great a lord is he!
3) And he grants them grace, and thus he said:
4) Though that she were a queen or princess.

5) Thy temple I will worship evermore
6) As keep me from your vengeance and your anger
7) I am, you know, yet of your company.
8) Now help me, lady, since you may and can.
9) You will be married to one of those.
10) Give me the victory, I ask you no more.

1) *his*
2) *he*
3) *hem*
4) *she*
5) *thy, I*
6) *thy, thyn*
7) *I, thou*
8) *me, ye*
9) *thou*
10) *me, I, thee*

✍ Exercise 18: Strong and Weak Verbs in Middle English

Strong: 2), 3), 5), 8), 9);   weak: 1), 4), 6), 7), 10)

✍ Exercise 19: The Peterborough Chronicle

"Then Eustace, the king's son, went to France and married the French king's sister. By this, he hoped to get hold of Normandy. But he was not successful as he was an evil man. Wherever he went, he did more evil than good. He robbed the lands and put great taxes on them. He brought his wife to England and put her in the castle of Canterbury. She was a good woman but she was not happy with him. And Christ did not want him to reign very long and therefore, both he and his mother died."

✍✍ Exercise 20: *Piers Plowman*

"In the season summer, when the sun was soft, I dressed with woolen clothes as if I was a sheep. In the habit of a hermit who is unholy in his works, I went forth into the world to hear wonders. And I saw many marvelous and strange things. But on a morning in May on the Malvern hills I fell asleep from the weariness of walking and as I lay in the field, I rested and slept; I dreamed marvelously as I will tell."

1) The letters ⟨i⟩ or ⟨y⟩ are used interchangeably. The letter ⟨y⟩ is in frequent use and also the use of ⟨y⟩ for the 1st person singular pronoun *I*. The letter ⟨v⟩ stands in initial position and ⟨u⟩ in medial position for both the vowel [ʊ], e.g. *unholy*, *spiritus*, and the consonant [v]. The diagraph ⟨wh⟩ is used for ⟨hw⟩, e.g. *whan*, *while*.

2) Old English long vowels were shortened in closed syllables, e.g. *softe, slepte*. The sound [j] was vocalized to [ɪ], e.g. *say, lay*. Old English [ɑ:] changed into [ɔ:], e.g. *vnholy*. Old English [æɑ] has assimilated to open [ɛ:], e.g. *estward*. The initial sequence [hl-] was simplified to [-l], e.g. *lened* (Old English *hleonian*).

3) Only three personal pronouns occur in this text: *hit, me,* and *y*.

4) The noun plurals have the *-es / -s* inflection (e.g. *shroudes*), except for *men*. Of the four present tense verb forms, *y may* and *y shal* are auxiliaries, *y leue* shows the 1st person singular suffix *-e*, and *þis world ascuth* the 3rd person singular more usually written ⟨eþ / -eth⟩; past tense verbs include both strong forms (e.g. *beheld, biful*), with a change of stem vowel, and weak forms (e.g. *lened, woned*) with the *-ed* suffix. The only past participle *of-walked* has the regular weak ⟨-ed⟩ suffix, and the present participle forms have the *-ing* suffix. The Old English *-an* infinitive has been reduced to *-e* (e.g. *slepe*). The only forms of the verb *be* in the text are the past forms *was* and *were*.

5) There is some inversion of elements such as *y a shep were, wondres to here*, and *lened y*. The only structures which do not exist in Present-day English are *me biful* and *me mette* (impersonal construction). The clause *y shope me into shroudes* ('I dressed myself in woolen clothes') contains an example of a reflexive verb with the pronoun *me*, which would require *myself* in Present-day English.

6) Most of the words are of Anglo-Saxon origin. There are some words from French (and hardly any from Old Norse).

examples		ME	examples		ME
OE	*sumor*	*somur*	OF	*hermite*	*heremite*
OF	*seson*	*sesoun*	OE	*weorc*	*werk*
OE	*sōfte*	*softe*	OE	*weorold*	*world*
OE	*sunne*	*sonne*	OE	*wundor*	*wonder*
OE	*scēap*	*shep*	OF	*mai*	*May*
OF	*abit*	*abite*	ON	*báir*	*bothe*

✍✍ Exercise 21: Geoffrey Chaucer's Prologue to the *Canterbury Tales*

1) "When April with his mild showers has soaked right through to the dry roots of March, and bathed every sap-vessel in moisture by the virtue of which the flower is produced; when Zephir with his sweet breath has also breathed on the delicate shoots of every grove and field, and the young sun has completed (the second) half of his course in the ram, and (when) small birds are singing, those that sleep all nights with eyes open, (as nature prompts them in their hearts); then folks long to go on pilgrimages (and palmers to foreign shores) to visit distant shrines,

well-known in many different lands, and especially, from the end of every shire
of England, they go to Canterbury, to visit the blessed martyr, who has helped
them whenever they were ill."

2) *droghte* ['drʊxtə] - [draʊt], *roote* ['roːtə] - [ruːt], *yonge* ['jʊŋgə] - [jʌŋ],
open ['ɔːpən] - ['əʊpən], *corages* [kʊ'raːdʒəs] - ['kʌrɪdʒ] (in RP)[2]

The following sound changes from Middle English to Present-day English can
be observed:

– [ʊx] > [uː], GVS [uː] > [aʊ]

– loss of [-ə] in ['roːtə] and GVS > Present-day English [ruːt]

– loss of final [g] after nasals and loss of [-ə], also [ʊ] > [ʌ]

– ['ɔːpən] Early Modern English GVS: [ɔː] > [oː] > [əʊ], thus ['əʊpən]

– stress shift to the first syllable; the reduced second syllable attains [ɪ] as its
nucleus

– unstressed [ɪ]; also [ʊ] > [ʌ]

3) Examples are *veyne*, *yonge*, *sonne*, *yronne*, and *sundry*.

4) Middle English *breeth* [brɛːθ] was shortened to Present-day English *breath*
[brɛθ]. Middle English *heeth* [hɛːθ] corresponds to Present-day English *heath*
[hiːθ]; this word underwent the GVS, thus [ɛː] > [eː] > [iː].

5) Examples are:

– French borrowing: *cours*, *corages*, *licour*, *melodye*, *vertu*

– loss of words (Middle English > Present-day English): *eek*, *kowthe*, *sondry*,
sundry

– meaning shift

Middle English		Present-day English	
licour	'liquid'	*liqueur*	'alcoholic drink'
seken	'visit'	*seek*	'look for sth'
straunge	'distant'	*strange*	'odd'
inspire	'to breathe in'	*inspire*	'encourage'
corage	'heart, feeling'	*courage*	'bravery'
seeke	'ill'	*sick*	'wanting to throw up' (BrE)

✍ Exercise 22: John Hart's *Orthographie*

1) Examples of 'abuses' of spelling are:
   – superfluous letters: *brought* ⟨ugh⟩, *reach* ⟨a⟩, *light* ⟨gh⟩
   – adaptation: **buty – beauty*, **curidge – courage*, ** yogert* - yoghurt, **sergent -
   sergeant*
   – difference: *flower – flour, flea – flee, key – quay, suite - sweet*

2) "In this title above-written, I consider of the ⟨i⟩ in exercise, & of the ⟨u⟩, in
   instruments: the like of the ⟨i⟩, in title, which the common man, and many
   learned, do sound in the diphthongs ⟨ei⟩, and ⟨iu⟩..." The described sound
   changes are part of the Great Vowel Shift.

✍✍ Exercise 23: Phonological History

	OE	ME	PdE
1)	['tiːma]	['tiːmə]	[taɪm]
2)	['ʏntʃə]	['ɪntʃə]	[ɪntʃ]
3)	['sɛᵊvɔn]	['sɛvən]	['sevən][3]
4)	['krabːa]	['krabːə]	[kræb]
5)	['hnʊtʊ]	['hnʊtə]	[nʌt]
6)	['hyːdɑn]	['hiːdən]	[haɪd]
7)	['tʃeːzə]	['tʃeːzə]	[tʃiːz]
8)	['hweːol]	['hweːl]	[wiːl]
9)	[dæːd]	[dɛːd]	[diːd]
10)	[sæː]	[sɛː]	[siː]
11)	[hæɑp]	[hɛːp]	[hiːp]
12)	[fuːl]	[fuːl]	[faʊl]
13)	['foːda]	['foːdə]	[fuːd]
14)	[haːm]	[hɔːm]	[həʊm]
15)	[jʊŋg]	[jʊŋg]	[jʌŋ]
16)	['kneːo]	[kneː]	[niː]
17)	['kʏsːɑn]	['kɪsːən]	[kɪs]
18)	['æɑst]	[ɛːst]	[iːst]
19)	[fæst]	[fast]	[fɑːst]
20)	[hluːd]	[hluːd]	[laʊd]
21)	['læːvɑn]	['lɛːvən]	[lɪːv]

22)	['sɑːpə]	['sɔːpə]	[səʊp]
23)	['stɑndɑn]	['stɑ(ː)ndən]	[stænd]
24)	['sʊnːə]	['sʊnːə]	[sʌn]
25)	[teːθ]	[teːθ]	[tiːθ]
26)	[dæj]	[dɛɪ]	[deɪ]

✍ Exercise 24: The Great Vowel Shift

1) Changes due to the Great Vowel Shift

example	Middle English	Present-day English
mice	[miːs]	[maɪs]
mouse	[muːs]	[maʊs]
geese	[geːs]	[giːs]
goose	[goːs]	[guːs]
break	['brɛːkən]	[breɪk]
broken	['brɔːken]	['brəʊkən]
name	['nɑːmə]	[neɪm]

2) Present-day English developments

1)	[ɔː]	[əʊ]	*boast*
2)	[oː]	[uː]	*brood*
3)	[aː]	[eɪ]	*dame*
4)	[ɛː]	[eɪ]	*great*
5)	[uː]	[aʊ]	*gown*
6)	[uː]	[uː]	*you*
7)	[aː]	[eɪ]	*case*
8)	[iː]	[aɪ]	*lice*
9)	[iː]	[aɪ]	*hide*
10)	[eː]	[iː]	*meet*
11)	[iː]	[aɪ]	*mine*
12)	[aː]	[eɪ]	*pace*
13)	[oː]	[uː]	*pool*
14)	[ɔː]	[əʊ]	*pole*
15)	[ɛː]	[iː]	*read*

16) [aː]	[eɪ]	*safe*
17) [uː]	[aʊ]	*out*
18) [iː]	[aɪ]	*wide*

✍✍ Exercise 25: Vowel changes

1) The vowel that developed from Middle English [a]

a) is [ɑː] in British English and [æ] in American English.
b) is [æ].
c) is [ɔː].
d) is [ɔː]. The [1] was vocalized.
e) is [æ] in American English, [ɑː] in British English. The [1] was dropped.
f) is [ɑː]. The [1] was dropped.
g) Before voiceless fricatives (exept for [ʃ]) British English has [ɑː], and American English [æ].

2) The vowel that developed from Middle English [ɔ]

a) is [ɒ] in British English and [ɔː] in American English.
b) is [ɒ] in British English and [ɑː] in American English.
c) is [əʊ].
d) is [ɒ] in British English and [ɑː] in American English.
e) While British English prefers using [ɒ], American English prefers [ɑː] or [ɔː].

3) The development of Middle English [ʊ]

a) is usually [ʊ] > [ʌ].
b) remained unchanged before [1].
c) An exception to the second generalization is *skull*.

4) The vowel [ɛː]

a) was shortened before the alveolars /t, d/, and before dentals and /k/ (at the end of the 16th century and in the 17th century).
b) In Present-day English, the Middle English sound [ɛː] became [iː].

✍ Exercise 26: Early Modern English Pronouns

1) The father uses *th*-forms to address his daughter, whereas she uses *y*-forms to show respect to her father.

2) The prince uses the polite *y*-forms to address the king but the king himself talks to the prince employing *th*-forms. (The king is superior to the prince.)

3) While King Claudius addresses Hamlet with the courteous *y*-form, Queen Gertrude urges Hamlet to forgo his mourning and to remain at the Danish court with *th*-forms. King Claudius shows respect, while Queen Gertrude talks to Hamlet as a mother.

✍✍ Exercise 27: Prepositions

   1) *on*
   2) *for*
   3) *of*
   4) *at*
   5) *over*
   6) *from*
   7) *about / of*
   8) *for*
   9) *out(side)*
  10) *on*

✍✍ Exercise 28: Margery Kempe

1) All the plural nouns are spelled with the suffix *–ys*: *teerys, sobbyngys, syhyngys, schamys, spytys*. This suggests that the inflection was still pronounced [ɪs] or [əs].

2) *hir* (3rd person singular possessive), *she* (1st person singular, subject), *I* (first person singular, subject), *it* (3rd person singular, subject).

3) The definite article is *þe*, the demonstrative *þis / thys*, and the indefinite article *a*, as in Present-day English.

4) The use of prepositions is identical to Present-day English usage (except perhaps for *on a nyght*): *aftyr, in, of, on, owt, to, wyth*. There are also compound prepositions: *þerwyth, wyth-owtyn*.

5) There are no significant differences here between Early Modern English and Present-day English. In general, however, many strong OE verbs became weak in their inflections during the Middle English and Early Modern English period. Examples of verb forms: *dede* (1st person singular), *lay, herd, þowt, styrt* (3rd person singular), *have* (infinitive), *dredyng* (present participle), *herd, ben* (past participle).

6) The complexities of the verb phrase gradually increase. Examples from the text: *might be herd* (modal + passive), *caused... for to haue* (infinitival clause).

7) In this text, the present-day order of clause elements seems to be fully established.

8) The principal spelling differences between this text and Present-day English are:

⟨y⟩	*nygth, with, synne, thys, aftyr, dredyng, wretchyd, comparyson*
⟨þ⟩	*þis, þe*
⟨sch⟩	*sche*
⟨ow⟩	*sownd, þowt, owt, wyth-owtyn*
⟨u⟩	*euyr, deuocyon*
⟨-e⟩	*bedde, dede, melodye, blysse*

✍ Exercise 29: King James Bible and the New English Bible

1) The letter ⟨u⟩ is used instead of ⟨v⟩ in *ouer, diuided, euen, draue, heauily*. In turn, the letter ⟨v⟩ stands for Present-day English ⟨u⟩, as in *vpon, vnto,* and *vs*. Some words contain an ⟨e⟩ at the end: *goe, backe, winde, passe, hoste, cloude, tooke*. The plural is ⟨es⟩ in *wheeles* (today ⟨s⟩ only). The usual 3rd person singular -*s* is written as ⟨eth⟩: *fighteth*. Two words are written with upper-case letters in the King James Bible but not in the New English Bible: *Sea, East*. The spelling ⟨'s⟩ for the genitive is not yet being used in the earlier text.

2) The different spellings of ⟨u, v⟩ are caused by different spelling conventions. At the beginning of a word ⟨v⟩ was used for either ⟨u⟩ or ⟨v⟩, and in the body of a word ⟨u⟩ was used for either. The ⟨e⟩ is added to words rather arbitrarily. The pronunciation of [ə] in final position was given up in Early Modern English (or even earlier). In the 16th century, [s] assimilated to [z] in voiced neighborhood (except after the voiced sibilants [ʒ] and [dʒ]). Therefore the Early Modern English pronunciation must have been [wi:lz], Middle English ['hwe:ləs]. The form -*eth* is a remnant from the south. (It seems to have been common especially in formal writing.) In Early Modern English, upper-case letters were commoner than today. They were also used for geographical terms. The spelling convention ⟨'s⟩ for the genitive became standard later (in the 17th century).

3) The coordinator *and* is used very often; it introduces the main clauses. This convention is given up in the New English Bible.

4) In the King James Bible, the conjunction *that* occurs more often, and has temporal and consequential meaning: "that in the morning watch" vs. "in the morning watch"; "that they droue them" vs. "and made them…"; "so that the Egyptians" (the same usage in both texts). In Present-day English, it can not be used with a temporal meaning, and when referring to a result, it is always *so… that*.

5) Compare: "vpon the dry ground" vs. "on the dry ground"; "vnto them" vs. "for them"; "looked vnto" vs. "looked down on". Apparently, *vnto* was a general preposition in Early Modern English that covered a whole range of prepositional uses. It has been replaced by *on*, *for*, and *down on*.

6) The word *draue* corresponds to Present-day English 'drove' (Old English *drāf*, Middle English *drof*). (According to Görlach, the spelling <a> is a hypercorrection.[4])

✍✍ Exercise 30: Shakespeare's *Romeo and Juliet*

1) The pronouns *thou*, *thy*, and *thee* were used by persons of higher rank addressing an inferior (Juliet addressing the nurse). The pronoun *you* was used by persons of lower rank to a superior (by the nurse, except for *thy* in the last line). The cases were *thou*: subject case, *thee*: object case, *thy*: possessive case, *you*: subject case.

2) Present-day English "I don't know" (*do*-support necessary in negative statements today).

3) "I would": main verb, meaning "I wish", today a modal verb (used in all kinds of contexts, for instance, as the past tense form of *will*).

4) The 2nd person singular form of *do*. The form *do* here means 'to do, to make' (not possible in Present-day English).

5) The form *hadst* is the 2nd person singular past tense subjunctive form of *have* meaning 'possess' (used as a main verb here). The auxiliary *be* also occurs in its subjunctive form here (3rd person singular / plural present tense).

6) Words
   - *aweary:* *1552, *a*-prefix + *weary*, 'tired, weary', no longer in use
   - *(give) leave*, from Old English, 'permission asked for', here: 'give me a minute's rest', obsolete today in this context (but compare *leave of absence*)
   - *fie*: from Middle English, an exclamation of indignance, no longer in use
   - *jaunce*: either from the verb, *1593, 'to prance as a horse', obsolete or dialectal, or from *jaunt*, *1592, 'a troublesome journey', still in use today
   - *nay*: from Old Norse, 'no', now archaic or dialectal
   - *stay (awhile, the circumstance)*: as an intransitive verb: 'to stand still', *1440, now rare; or transitive, 'to wait for', *1586, now archaic
   - *(say) either*: from Old English, used as a pronoun, 'one or the other of two'
   - *compare* (noun): *1589, 'comparison', dated
   - *warrant*: from Middle English, 'to guarantee as true, "I am sure of it", dated
   - *wench*: from Middle English, 'young woman', now dialectal

   From the 16th century are *aweary*, *jaunce / jaunt*, *stay* (transitive), and *compare*.

✍✍ Exercise 31: British and American Vocabulary

1)	*engineer*	13)	*hood*
2)	*car*	14)	*windshield*
3)	*truck*	15)	*trunk*
4)	*overpass*	16)	*muffler*
5)	*(railroad) tie*	17)	*storage battery*
6)	*highway*	18)	*license plate*
7)	*station wagon*	19)	*suspenders*
8)	*trailer*	20)	*wrench*
9)	*rowboat*	21)	*sneakers*
10)	*sailboat*	22)	*trashcan*
11)	*bathing suit*	23)	*phone booth*
12)	*baggage*	24)	*mail box*

Mock Exams

Test 1

1. Germanic and Old English

1) Which sound law is said to be responsible for the change from [t] to [θ] in Latin *tres* and English *three*?

2) Explain the following sound variants:

   a) irregular plural: *fōt, fēt* ('foot', 'feet')
   b) weak verb: *þencan, þōhte, geþōht* ('think', 'thought', 'thought')

3) The Old English sounds [h], [ç], and [x] were allophones of one phoneme. In which position did each allophone occur? (See, for example, *hof* ('building'), *drihten* ('lord'), and *dohtor* ('daughter').)

4) Which Old English letters used in Old English handwriting were not taken from the Latin alphabet?

5) Give one orthographic, one phonological, one morphological, and one syntactic difference between the beginning of the Lord's Prayer in Old English and Present-day English.
   Fæder ūre, þū þe eart on heofonum, sī þīn nama gehālgod.

6) Borrowing from Latin occurred on three distinct occasions before the end of the Old English period. Which were these? Give examples.

2. Middle English

1) What were the main dialects in Middle English?

2) Which dialect became the standard variety of English? Why?

3) Transcribe the sounds in the following words: *knyght* ('knight'), *ryde* ('ride'), *deuise* ('devise'), and *seruysable* ('serviceable'). Explain also the use of the letters ⟨y⟩ and ⟨u⟩ in Middle English.

4) Why are there different vowels in the following pairs of words today?
   keep – kept; read – read (past tense), *feel – felt*

5) Summarize the development of the personal pronoun system from Old English to Middle English.

6) What role did Latin loanwords play in Middle English?

3. Early Modern English and Present-day English

1) What were the aims of the 18th century prescriptive grammarians?

2) In what way does the spelling of unstressed syllables in English fail to represent accurately the pronunciation?

3) Give the Present-day English phonetic transcription (RP) of the following Middle English words and explain the relevant sound changes that took place from Middle English to Present-day English.

ME		ME transcription
lif	'life'	[liːf]
maken	'make'	['maːkən]
bone	'bone'	['bɔːnə]
glæd	'glad'	[glad]
lawe	'law'	['lauə]
took	'took'	[toːk]
word	'word'	[wʊrd]

4) In Early Modern English, adjectives could form comparatives with *-er* and *-est*, and / or *more* and *most*. What are the rules for the comparative forms today?

Consider the following Early Modern English sentences and describe the type of deviation from current usage.

a) *So, now it is more surer on my head.* (Marlowe, 1 *Tamburlaine* 2.7.65)
b) *Much greater griefe and shamefuller regret* (Spenser, *Faerie Queene* 4.11.15.4)
c) *Silence is the perfectest Herault of ioy.* (*Much Ado About Nothing* 2.1.317)
d) *To take the basest, and most poorest shape* (*King Lear* 2.3.7)
e) *Ingratitude, more strong then Traitors armes* (*Julius Caesar* 3.2.189)

5) What were *inkhorn terms*, and why were they ridiculed?

6) What accounts for the high degree of uniformity in American English?

Test 2

1. Germanic and Old English

1) What is a *language family*? To which branch of Germanic does English belong?

2) Give an example of i-mutation, and explain the process involved.

3) Give the sound law that accounts for *þ* vs. *d* in *snīþan, snāþ, snidon, sniden* ('to cut', German *schneiden*). Explain.

4) What is the difference between weak and strong verbs? Give examples.

5) Transcribe the pronunciation of the underlined letters: *agan* ('to owe'), *arcebiscop* ('archbishop'), *deofol* ('devil'), *lecgan* ('lay').

6) What were the sources of Old English vocabulary?

2. Middle English

1) Which languages were spoken in the Middle English period and by whom? Why did the language of the dominant culture (superstratum) decline in the course of time?

2) Which new spelling conventions influenced the traditional written form of Old English? What problem occurred when the spelling changed from Old English to Middle English, and how was it solved?

3) Transcribe the following Middle English words. What sound changes are responsible for the discrepancies between Old English and Middle English?

Old English		OE transcription	Middle English
cyssan	'to kiss'	[ˈkʏsːɑn]	*kissen*
fæste	'fast'	[ˈfæstə]	*faste*
hēap	'heap'	[hæɑp]	*hepe*
dæg	'day'	[dæj]	*day*
haldan	'to hold'	[ˈhɑldɑn]	*holden*
nama	'name'	[ˈnɑmɑ]	*name*

4) Which two methods of indicating the plural of nouns remained common in Middle English?

5) Give the personal endings of the indicative of verbs in Middle English.

6) Many of the Middle English loanwords from French reflect the cultural and political dominance of the Normans. Explain this statement and give some examples of French loanwords.

3. Early Modern English and Present-day English

1) In the 16th century many English people considered English spelling to be chaotic. Explain why. What was done in order to stabilize orthography?

2) What kinds of phonological changes were caused by the phoneme /r/ in Modern English?

3) The Present-day English vowel [i:] can be spelled ⟨ea⟩ (*meat*), ⟨ee⟩ (*meet*), and ⟨ie⟩ (*niece, field*). Explain.

4) Which two constructions of the verb system have become increasingly common during the Modern English period? How did they develop?

5) Which foreign languages contributed to the English word stock during the 18th century and why? Give examples.

6) Is American English more or less conservative than British English? Does the answer that applies to pronunciation also apply to vocabulary?

Solutions to the Mock Exams

Solutions to Test 1

1. Germanic and Old English

1) Grimm's Law: *bh, dh, gh* > *b, d, g*, and *p, t, k* > *f, þ, χ*, and *b, d, g* > *p, t, k*

2) Explanation of sound variants:

a) I-mutation in the plural ([foːt] > [fœːt] > [feːt], from **fōt-iz*)

b) Infinitive with i-mutation (**þank-jan* > *þencan* ['θɛntʃan] (palatalization of [k] > [tʃ] in the neighborhood of front vowels). Past tense [k] + dental suffix [t] > [xt], further loss of [n] before [x] + nasalization, and lengthening of the vowel, thus ['θɔːxtə])

3) The letter ⟨h⟩ is pronounced [h] word-initially, as in Old English *hof* [hɔf], [x] in the neighborhood of back vowels elsewhere, thus Old English ['dɔxtɔr], [ç] in the neighborhood of front vowels elsewhere, thus Old English ['drɪçtən].

4) The letters ⟨þ⟩ and ⟨ƿ⟩ were taken from the runic alphabet. The letters ⟨æ⟩ and ⟨ð⟩ are both derived from Latin.

5) Differences:

a) Orthographic differences: The letters ⟨þ⟩ and ⟨æ⟩ are used in the text.

b) Phonological differences: The Old English word *fæder* ['fædər] is pronounced ['fɑːθə] in Present-day English (RP). Furthermore, Old English *ūre* ['uːrə] is now *our* ['aʊə], and Old English *nama* ['nɑmɑ] is now *name* [neɪm].

c) Morphological differences: the Present-day English personal pronoun *you* has the forms *þīn* (genitive singular), *þū* (nominative singular), and *þē* (accusative-dative singular) in Old English. Further inflected forms in the text are: *ūre* (1ˢᵗ person genitive plural), *heofonum* (dative plural).

d) Syntactic differences: reversed order of pronoun and noun: *Fæder ūre* (today *our father*, from Latin *pater noster*); word arrangement of *sī þīn nama gehālgod* ⟺ *hallowed be your name*. In Old English, the object could stand between the auxiliary and the main verb.

6) Firstly, there was continental borrowing. The Germanic tribes had already met the Romans on the continent. Borrowings from this period are: *weall* ('wall'), *cēap* ('cheap'), and *mynet* ('coin'). Secondly, Latin was transmitted through Celtic. The Celts had adopted Latin words, for instance *ceaster* ('camp'), *munt* ('mountain'), and *port* ('harbor'). Thirdly, the Christianization of Britain

resulted in a significant number of new Latin borrowings, for instance *abbud* ('abbot'), *engel* ('angel'), *psalm*, and *nunne* ('nun').

2. Middle English

1) Five principal dialects of Middle English can be distinguished, namely: Southern, Kentish, East Midland, West Midland and Northern. Southern and Kentish were spoken south of the Thames, East and West Midland between the Humber and the Thames, and the Northern dialect north of the Humber.

2) The dialect spoken by the merchant class in London became the standard variety of English. The merchants spoke the East Midland dialect that had already developed to a class dialect within London by the 14th century. During the 15th century, a written standard also began to emerge, which by the end of the 16th century had been accepted as the written standard in general, under the influence of several criteria:

   – Since the court was in London after the Norman conquest, London became the social, political, and commercial center. People from the East Midlands and from other parts of Britain migrated to London in order to trade and to work.
   – In 1476 the printing press was set up in London.
   – The East Midland dialect occupied an intermediate position between the north and the south.
   – The East Midlands was also the largest and most populous of the major dialectal areas.
   – The two universities of Oxford and Cambridge were situated in the East Midland dialectal area. They not only contributed to the prestige of the East Midland dialect, but also stimulated mobility.

3) [knɪçt], ['riːdə], [də'viːzə], [servɪ'zaːblə] (or [servɪ'saːblə])

   Besides ⟨i⟩, the letter ⟨y⟩ is also used for [ɪ] and [iː] in Middle English texts. This convention is connected to the so-called minim problem. In the continental Carolingian handwriting, the letters ⟨i⟩, ⟨u⟩, ⟨n⟩, ⟨m⟩, and ⟨w⟩ looked so similar that they could easily be confused. Consequently, the unambiguous ⟨y⟩ was often used instead of ⟨i⟩. The letter ⟨u⟩ was also used for [v].

4) The three verbs are all weak, recognizable by the dental suffix in the past tense. However, today these verbs are considered irregular. Around the year 1000, stressed long vowels were shortened before consonant sequences (except before *mb*, *nd*, *ld*, and *rd*). Thus Old English *cēpte* ('kept') was shortened to *kepte*, *rǣdde* to *redde* / *radde*, and *fēlde* to *felte*. In Early Modern English, the long vowels also underwent the Great Vowel Shift: [eː] > [iː], as in *keep* and *feel*, and [ɛː] > [eː] > [iː], as in *read* (infinitive). This is why the originally weak verbs are now irregular.

5) The following main developments in the personal pronoun system occurred during the transition from Old English to Middle English:

a) The dative and accusative forms merged into one form (e.g. Old English singular dative masculine *him*, singular accusative masculine *hine* > Middle English singular dative / accusative masculine *him*).

b) The dual was abandoned.

c) The forms of the 3rd person plural were replaced by Scandinavian pronouns. Firstly, the 3rd person plural nominative *hī(e)* was replaced by *they* (Old Norse *þeir*); later 3rd person plural genitive was also replaced by *their* (Old Norse *þeirra*), and 3rd person plural dative / accusative by them (Old Norse *þeim*). Thus Old English *hī(e), hira, him, hī(e)* changed into *they* (*here*) / *their* (*hem*) / *them*.

d) The new feminine singular nominative *she* developed (perhaps from a special phonetic development of the older *hēo*).

6) During the Middle English period, and especially in the 14th and 15th centuries, many Latin words were borrowed by English. The role of Latin borrowings was of course not as important as that of the French, but Latin was still considered highly prestigious, especially among churchmen and scholars, who could not only read and write but also speak it. The Latin borrowings were mainly taken from the areas of religion, law, arts, and science. (However, it is not always clear whether a word was borrowed from French or Latin.) The words generally gained admission through the written language. Sometimes they were also used for stylistic reasons.

3. Early Modern English and Present-day English

1) In the rationalistic spirit of the time, it was desired by learned men to give English a pure and permanent form. An English Academy was called for, which was to take care of the codification of the language. English was thought to be corrupt and in need of improvement and standardization. However, the academy was never founded (Some scholars doubted whether language change could be held back by rules, and moreover, the most powerful supporter and sponsor – Queen Anne – died in 1714.). Instead, the codification of the language was mainly done by individuals, who wrote dictionaries and grammar books. Examples are: *A Dictionary of the English Language* (1755) by Samuel Johnson, and grammar books by Joseph Priestley, (1761), Robert Lowth (1762), James Buchanan (1762), and John Ash (1763). In North America, the spelling book (1783) and the grammar (1784) written by Noah Webster contributed to the codification of an American language.

2) Due to the reduction of unstressed vowels, the Middle English inflectional endings were reduced to [ə]. Subsequently, the remaining unstressed vowels

were further reduced. At the beginning of words, unaccented syllables were reduced to [ə] or [ɪ]. In final position, they were often lost.

Examples are:

Middle English		Present-day English	
agreen	[a'gre:ən]	*agree*	[ə'gri:]
departen	[də'partən]	*depart*	[dɪ'pɑ:t]
observaunce	[ˌɔbsər'vɑunsə]	*observance*	[əb'zɜ:vəns]

Due to these and other changes, and also to the writing conventions of the Norman scribes, the spelling of unaccented syllables today does not match pronunciation. Examples are the loss of *r* in *care* [keə], Middle English ['ka:rə]; and words such as *consent* [kən'sent] for Middle English *consenten* [kʊn'sɛntən].

3) Transcription

Present-day English	sound change(s)
[laɪf]	GVS: [i:] > [əi] > [aɪ]
[meɪk]	GVS: [a:] > [ɛ:] > [eɪ]
[bəʊn]	GVS: [ɔ:] > [oʊ] > [əʊ]
[glæd]	short [a] > [æ]
[lɔ:]	monophthongization: [ɑʊ] > [ɔ:]
[tʊk]	GVS: [o:] > [u:], and shortening of [u:]
[wɜ:d]	vocalization of [r], and [ʊ] + [ə] > [ɜ:]

4) In Present-day English the forms of the comparative and superlative of adjectives depend on the number of syllables in the uninflected form. In general, monosyllabic adjectives and also many disyllabic adjectives take the endings *-er* and *-est* (*big – bigger – biggest, narrow – narrower – narrowest*). Most adjectives with three or more syllables (and also many with two), adjectives ending in *-ing* and *-ed*, and adjectives containing any suffix except *-ly* or *-y* form the comparative and superlative with *more* and *most* (*difficult – more difficult – most difficult, interesting – more interesting – most interesting, afraid – more afraid – most afraid, helpful – more helpful – most helpful*).

Type of deviation:

a) double comparative, in Present-day English *surer* (monosyllabic adjective)
b) comparative *-er* , in Present-day English *more shameful* (disyllabic adjective with suffix *-ful*)
c) superlative *-est*, in Present-day English *most perfect* (disyllabic adjective)
d) double superlative, in Present-day English *poorest* (monosyllabic adjective)
e) comparative *more*, in Present-day English *stronger* (monosyllabic adjective)

5) In the Renaissance there was a need for new English words, especially in the areas of science and technology. Furthermore, the study of classical and other literature led scholars to introduce words from these sources into English. Some people strongly objected to these new words, especially if they were overused. They considered them to be alien, artificial and obscure, and called them *inkhorn terms*. Some writers even tried to reintroduce obsolete Middle English words, also then called *Chaucerisms*. However, the borrowing of new words could not be halted. Some Renaissance examples from Latin and Greek are: *encyclopedia*, *idiosyncracy*, *lexicon*, *monopoly*, *transcribe*, and *necessitate*.

6) In the 17th century, the first permanent settlements took place in North America. The southern settlers of Virginia had mainly come from the west of England, where the [r] was strongly pronounced after vowels. The northern settlers of New England mostly came from the east of England, and they lacked post-vocalic [r], which is still a feature of New England speech. During the 17th and 18th centuries large numbers of new immigrants from all over England, Northern Ireland, and Scotland arrived. They chose a place of residence or traveled further on, and they met others who had all kinds of accents. This caused the divisions between the various dialects to become blurred. Even later, immigrants poured in from all over the world, contributing further to the smoothing of distinctive accents. The result is a rather homogeneous American standard, apart from a few exceptions, such as the postvocalic [r].

Solutions to Test 2

1. Germanic and Old English

1) A language family is a group of languages that evolved from the same common source. The English language belongs to the West Germanic branch of the Indo-European languages.

2) An example of i-mutation is the noun *strength* (vs. the adjective *strong*). The nominalizing suffix *-iþu converted adjectives to nouns and caused i-mutation, which consisted of the raising or fronting of a vowel by assimilation to an *i* or *j* in the following syllable. Thus we have Old English *strong*, *strength*. There had also originally been an *i* in the comparative and superlative inflectional endings of some adjectives, so that we also have i-mutation in Old English *strenger* ('stronger') and *strengest* ('strongest').

3) The answer is Grimm's Law and Verner's Law. According to Grimm's Law, Indo-European *t* became Germanic *þ*. Since *snidon* and *sniden* originally had the accent on the second syllable, the voiceless fricative became voiced according to

Verner's Law and subsequently [d]. In *snīþan*, the fricative was pronounced [ð], because it occurred between two vowels: ['sni:ðan]. However, in the word *snāþ* it was pronounced as the voiceless counterpart of [ð], since here it occurred in final position: [sna:θ].

4) Weak verbs were Germanic verbs that formed their past tense by adding a dental suffix, for example Old English *swīgian, swīgode* (3rd person singular past tense), 'to be silent', German *schweigen*; or Old English *fetian, fetod* (past participle), 'fetch'.

Strong verbs were Germanic verbs that formed their past tense by ablaut of the stem vowel, for example *drīfan, drāf, drifon, drifen* (class I), 'to drive'; or *bindan, band, bundon, bunden* (class III), 'to bind'. Weak and strong does not necessarily correspond to regular and irregular. For instance, the verb *think* (*thought, thought*) is called an irregular verb, though it is a Germanic weak verb. Here the change of the stem vowel is not caused by ablaut but by certain sound changes.

5) Pronunciation

a) [ɣ]: ⟨g⟩ is pronounced as a voiced velar fricative in the neighborhood of back vowels.

b) [tʃ]: ⟨c⟩ is pronounced as a voiceless affricate in the neighborhood of front vowels.

c) [v]: ⟨f⟩ is pronounced voiced intervocalically.

d) [dʒ]: ⟨cg⟩ is pronounced as a voiced affricate in front of originally following [j], which caused consonant doubling (*lagjan*).

6) The following languages contributed to the word stock of the English language:

a) Celtic, as a result of the Anglo-Saxon conquest. A small number of words remain, being mostly place names: *Kent, Cornwall, London, Dover*.

b) Latin, either from the continent, or through Celtic transmission, or in the course of Christianization (from 597 onwards). Old English examples are: *butere* ('butter'), *candel* ('candle'), *scol* ('school'), *mynster* ('minster').

c) Scandinavian, in the course of the Scandinavian raids and settlements in Britain (8th to 11th centuries). Late Old English examples are *til* ('till'), *cnīf* ('knife'), *wrang* ('wrong'), *tacan* ('to take').

d) Greek, either directly, mostly by the Goths, or indirectly via Latin. Old English examples are *dēofol* ('devil'), *engel* ('angel'), *cirice* ('church'). The latter are two indirect borrowings.

e) French, due to the close contact between the English court of Edward the Confessor (1042-1066) and Normandy. Late Old English examples are: *prūd* ('proud'), and possibly *castel* ('castle') and *capun* ('capon', castrated cock).

2. Middle English

1) English was spoken by the common people, and French at the court, by the nobility and their personnel, and by government officials. Latin was used by churchmen and scholars. Several factors contributed to the decline of the language of the conquerors:

a) In the 13th century Normandy was lost to the French king, which resulted in the separation of the French and Anglo-Norman nobility. Due to the 100 years' war between France and England, the gap between the two countries widened even more.

b) Due to the growing contact between the Anglo-Norman nobility and the English population (trading, intermarriage), English became generally used among the upper classes.

c) In comparison to the French used in Paris, the French of the Anglo-Normans was increasingly considered to be rustic and antiquated.

d) During Late Middle English the conditions of the working classes were improving, and a middle class with growing national feeling emerged. Thus English became more and more prestigious.

e) The Bible was translated into English, and many authors chose to write in English.

2) The *insular hand* was the usual form of Old English writing until the 11th century, when the Norman scribes introduced the writing style called *Carolingian minuscule*. While the insular hand was a more angular and cursive style with rounded, flowing strokes, the Carolingian minuscule mainly consisted of a sequence of vertical strokes. As a consequence, adjacent letters formed by such strokes (⟨u, n, m, v⟩) were difficult to read. This difficulty has been called the *minim problem*. In order to distinguish the different letters, the Norman scribes introduced ⟨o⟩ for ⟨u⟩ and ⟨y⟩ for ⟨i⟩.

Furthermore the French scribes introduced some other spelling conventions, such as ⟨ch⟩ for Old English ⟨c⟩ when this was pronounced [tʃ], ⟨k⟩ for [k], ⟨qu⟩ for Old English ⟨cw⟩, and ⟨ou⟩ for Old English ⟨u⟩ when this was pronounced [u:]. Examples are:

Old English		Middle English	
cēosan	'to choose'	*chesen*	['tʃe:zən]
cēpan	'to keep'	*kepen*	['ke:pən]
cwēn	'queen'	*queen*	[kwe:n]

From the 14th century onwards, the spelling was also influenced by the writing conventions of the chancery, called *Chancery hand*. For instance, the chancery wrote *not* (and not *nat*), *such* (and not *sich* or *swiche*), and *could* (instead of *koude*).

3) Transcription

ME transcription	sound change(s)
['kɪsːən]	unrounding of [ʏ] > [ɪ]
['fastə]	[æ] > [a]
[hɛːp]	monophthongization: [æɑ] > [ɛː]
[dɛɪ]	new diphthong: [æ] + [j] > [ɛɪ]
['hɔːldən]	lengthening before -ld and [ɑː] > [ɔː]
['naːmə]	lengthening in open syllables: [ɑ] > [aː]

+ reduction of unstressed syllables in *kissen*, *holden*, and *name* (> [ə])

4) The nominative accusative plural ending -*as* of the strong masculine *a*-stem became a pattern for the plural of most nouns in Middle English. As a result of the reduction of unstressed syllables, Old English -*as* developed into -(*e*)*s* in Middle English. In the south, the zero ending of the weak neuter *a*-stem and other ambiguous endings were also replaced by -(*e*)*n*, which is derived from the nominative accusative plural -*an* of the *n*-stem. Similarly to -*as*, the ending -*an* was reduced to -(*e*)*n*.

5) The Middle English verbs indicate person, number, mood, and tense in their inflectional endings:

– Person: 1st, 2nd, 3rd
– Number: singular, plural
– Mood: indicative, subjunctive, imperative
– Tense: present, past

Furthermore, there are strong and weak verbs. In ME their inflectional endings only differ with respect to singular past tense and past participle. The personal endings of ME weak verbs in the indicative were:

Singular	Indicative	
Person	Present Tense	Past Tense
1.	-*e*	-*e*
2.	-*es*, -*est*	-*est*
3.	-*es*, -*eth*	-*e*
Plural	-*es*, -*en*, -*eth*	-*en*

The ending -*es* (2nd and 3rd person singular) was used in the north, while -*est* (1st person singular) and -*eth* (3rd person singular) were used in the midlands and the south. The present tense plural had three variants: -*es* in the north, -*en* in the midlands, and -*eth* in the south.

The singular past tense forms of the strong verbs were Ø, -e and Ø for 1st, 2nd and 3rd person respectively; see for instance *band, bounde, band* ('to bind', strong verb) vs. *hopede, hopedest, hopede* ('to hope', weak verb).

In Middle English the Old English inflectional endings were reduced, and the distinctions between the conjugations were lost. Only the form 3rd person singular present tense has survived as an inflectional indicative verbal ending until today, derived from the northern Middle English ending *-(e)s*.

6) After the Norman conquest French became the language of the court, the nobility, and the administration (lay and spiritual). For this reason many words in the areas of politics, warfare, law, and religion were borrowed from French. Examples are the Present-day English words *government, court, tax, office; army, navy, enemy; justice, crime, prison;* and *prayer, dean, creator.* The upper classes also introduced words dealing with fashion, meals, and lifestyle, for instance, *fashion, garment, buckle; salmon, sardine, oyster;* and *curtain, cushion, park.* In addition, their cultural and intellectual interests are mirrored by the loanwords *art, painting, poet, romance, medicine,* and *physician.*

French was not only the language of the conquerors, it was also considered highly prestigious in Europe. It was a symbol for cultivation, and this is another reason why so many French words were assimilated into English.

3. Early Modern English and Present-day English

1) In the 16th century no standard spelling existed. The authors from the various dialectal areas spelled certain words differently. Moreover, due to certain sound changes, spelling conventions introduced by the Norman scribes, and heavy borrowing of French words, one letter could represent more than one sound, and vice versa. Consequently, many people considered English spelling to be inconsistent and unreliable. In order to change this, attempts were made to set up rules and devise more orderly spelling systems. During the 16th century a number of spelling books were written, for instance by John Hart in 1570, and Richard Mulcaster in 1582. While Hart tried to change spelling according to pronunciation, Mulcaster relied on current usage. By 1650 spelling had become more or less standardized in British English.

2) In the 17th and 18th centuries, postvocalic [r] was vocalized to [ə]. This development led to various sound changes, including the rise of the Present-day English centering diphthongs. In general, the short vowels [ɛ], [ɪ], [ʊ] before a former [r] changed to [ɜ:], and the loss of [r] before the long vowels [e:], [a:] / [ɛ:] and [o:] resulted in the respective centering diphthongs [ɪə], [eə], and [ʊə]. In recent English, [ʊə] has developed further into [ɔ:]. See the following examples (RP):

Middle English		Present-day English		sound change(s)
werk	[wɛrk]	*work*	[wɜːk]	[ɛ] + [r] > [ɜː]
stiren	['stɪrən]	*stir*	[stɜː]	[ɪ] + [r] > [ɜː]
spare	['spaːrə]	*hurt*	[hɜːt]	[ʊ] + [r] > [ɜː]
hurten	['hʊrtən]	*hear*	[hɪə]	[eː] + [r] > [ɪə]
heren	['heːrən]	*spare*	[speə]	[aː] + [r] > [eə]
beere	['bɛːrə]	*bear*	[beə]	[ɛː] + [r] > [eə]
pore	[poːr]	*poor*	[pʊə], [pɔː]	[oː] + [r] > [ʊə] > [ɔː]

3) In Middle English *meet* was pronounced ['meːtən] (*meten*). Due to the Great Vowel Shift, [eː] was raised to [iː], thus Present-day English [miːt]. In Middle English, *meat* was pronounced ['mɛːtə] (*mete*). Due to the Great Vowel Shift, [ɛː] was first raised to [eː], and later to [iː]. This is why *meet* and *meat* are homophones today.

In Early Modern English, ⟨ie⟩ was increasingly used for [iː]. At first, it was only used for the [iː] that had developed from the [eː] of Anglo-Norman loanwords (*niece*), but later also for native words (*field*). (The Old French diphthong [ɪə] had become [eː] in Anglo-Norman). Long [eː] underwent the Great Vowel Shift, thus [eː] > [iː].

4) The present perfect (and past perfect) and the progressive
From the 15th century onwards, the present perfect became more and more common. It was constructed by taking a form of *be* (intransitive verbs) or *have* (transitive verbs) and the past participle of a main verb. Later, *be* yielded to *have* in all cases.

The use of the progressive increased from the 14th century onwards, but it was optional until the 18th century. It developed from a form of the auxiliary *be* and a present participle. Its use was also influenced by the merger of the participle and the verbal noun in late Middle English.

5) After the Norman conquest French borrowings entered the English lexicon in great numbers; during the Renaissance the English vocabulary grew again owing to the influx of Latin and Greek loanwords. While these periods represent the peaks of borrowing activity in the history of the English language, the borrowing of words continued during later centuries. The 18th century was shaped by empirism and rationalism, geographic discoveries, scientific inventions, European politics, trade and lifestyle, and colonial expansion. Examples of borrowings at this time are:

French:	*glacier, ravine, plateau, picnic, bureau, bouillon*
Latin:	*insomnia, inertia, silicon, platinum, emanation*
Italian:	*allegro, concerto, loggia, lava*
German:	*pumpernickel, quartz, iceberg, waltz*
Russian:	*balalaika, parka*

British colonalism resulted in loanwords being adopted from the following languages:

Native American languages:	*moccasin, raccoon, squaw*
Urdu and Hindi:	*jungle, swami, loot*
Spanish and Portuguese: (Mexico, South America, Cuba)	*adobe, chili, coyote, verandah*

6) General American has kept some phonetic features of Shakespearean English, such as [æ] in e.g. *fast, last, bath,* and postvocalic [r]. It also kept a few of the older words and meanings, such as *sick* ('unwell'), or *fall* (British English *autumn*). However, the number of new words is much higher. American English is highly innovative with respect to vocabulary, and many Americanisms have been borrowed into other modern forms of English. Examples of Americanisms are: *tag line* ('punch line'), *boost* ('a push from behind'), *sassy* ('cheeky'), *flunk* ('fail an exam'), *round trip* (adj.), and *gas station* ('petrol station').

Overview of English Literature until 1700

1. From the First Written Records on (7th c.): A Classification According to Subject Matter[4]

Poetry is set out like prose and not in separate lines in the way we are used to.

1) Poems Treating Heroic Subject	*Beowulf* (poem of some 3,000 lines; folk epic), *The Battle of Finnsburh, Waldere, Widsith*
2) Historic Poems	*The Battle of Maldon, The Battle of Brunanburh*
3) Biblical Paraphrases and Reworkings of Biblical Subjects	after the 9th c.: *The Metrical Psalms, Genesis* and *Exodus, Christ, Judith* and the poems of the Junius MS
4) Lives of Saints	after the 9th c.: *Andreas, Elene, Guthlac, Juliana*

5) Other Religious Poems	– *The Phoenix, The Panther, The Whale* – the runic inscriptions on the Ruthwell Cross: part of a poem called *The Dream of the Rood* (probably 8th c.) – *Hymn* (one of the earliest English poems) by Cædmon (the earliest English poet whose name we know); the West Saxon version is found in the Old English translation of *Bede's Ecclesiastical History of the English People* (written in Latin and finished in AD 730); we have also an older Northumbrian version in the Latin text
6) Short Elegies and Poems	after the 9th c.: *The Wife's Lament, The Husband's Message, The Ruin, The Wanderer, The Seafarer*
7) Riddles and Gnomic Verse	
8) Miscellaneous	*Charms, The Runic Poem, The Riming Poem*

Prose appears later because verse is more effective for oral delivery and more easily retained in memory; Alfred the Great is the reason why England possessed a considerable body of prose literature in the ninth century; he had essential books translated or translated the books himself.

1) The Anglo-Saxon Chronicle	
2) The Translations of Alfred and his Circle	– *De Consolatione Philosophiae of Boethius* – *Soliloquia* of Saint Augustine – Moreover, the Old English version of Bede's *Ecclesiastical History* has been arranged by Alfred. – Alfred also instructed a record to be compiled of the important events of English history, past and present, and this, as continued for more than two centuries after his death, is the well-known *Anglo-Saxon Chronicle.*
3) Homiletic Writings	The most significant of these are: – *The Blickling Homilies*, 971 – Aelfric's *Catholic Homilies*, 990-992 and *Lives of the Saints*, 993-998 – *The Homilies* of Wulfstan

4) Other Religious Prose	This includes translations of portions of both the Old and New Testament, and a version of the Benedictine Office and Rule.
5) Prose Fiction (Translations from Latin)	*Apollonius of Tyre* *Alexander's Letter to Aristotle* *The Wonders of the East*
6) Scientific and Medical Writing	
7) Laws, Charters, and Wills	

2. From 1066 on (Middle English and Early Modern English): A Chronological Classification[6]

from	Poetry
12th c.	We find a considerable body of French literature being produced in England.
until 1154	The *Anglo-Saxon-Chronicle* was continued at Peterborough under the new title *Peterborough Chronicle*.
ca. 1200	*Ormulum*: written by the monk Orm
1250-1420	in the East Midland dialect: *Sir Orfeo*
1250-1420	*Lyrics* (14th c.) *The Cloud of Unknowing* (late 14th c.) *Saint Erkenwald* (in the West Midland dialect)
1350-1400	Period of Great Individual Writers – Geoffrey Chaucer (~1340-1400), greatest poet before Shakespeare; best known work: *Canterbury Tales* – William Langland's *Piers Plowman* (1362-1387) – an unknown author who wrote some of the finest poetry: *Sir Gawain and the Green Knight* (ca. 1384), *Patience* (both in the West Midland dialect) – John Gower: *Confessio Amantis* (written in the South East dialect)
15th c.	Imitative Period / Transition Period: Poetry was written in emulation of Chaucer. (by: Lydgate, Hoccleve, Skelton, Hawes, Henryson, Dunbar, Gawin Douglas, Lindsay)

from	Poetry
1608-1674	John Milton's greatest work: *Paradise Lost*
1631-1700	John Dryden, one of the great writers (poet and dramatist) in the English literary tradition

from	Prose
1150-1250	religious record: written in the West Midland Dialect – *Ancrene Riwle* (= *Wisse*), Layamon's *Brut* (ca. 1205), written in the South East Dialect: *The Owl and the Nightingale* (ca. 1195)
1250-1420	mystery plays, e.g. the York Cycle of 48 plays (late 14th c.)
1420-1430	English letters first occur among the Paston letters and in the Stonor correspondence between 1420 and 1430.
1450	Writing letters in English is the rule everywhere.
1350-1400	– John Wycliffe (died in 1384): putative translator of the Bible and author of a large and influential body of controversial prose – John Trevisa: *Dialogue between a Lord and a Clerk* (1385), written in the South West dialect
1460-1470	Sir Thomas Malory wrote legends about King Arthur, e.g.: *The Tale of King Arthur.*
1531	Sir Thomas Elyot's *The Gouvernour*
1678	John Bunyan (1628-1688): *The Pilgrim's Progress* (1678) – the language is close to colloquial everyday speech of the 1670s.

Notes:

[1] *Beowulf*, translated by Seamus Heaney 1999: 4.

[2] The transcription of the beginning of the *Prologue* can be found in Gimson/Cruttenden [5]1994: 73/74.

[3] The transcriptions [e] and [ɛ] stand for the same sound (cf. various English dictionaries).

[4] See Görlach 1978: 91f.

[5] Based on Mitchell/Robinson [5]1992: 141-143.

[6] Based on Baugh /Cable [4]1994: 151-153.

GLOSSARY

Ablaut → *Gradation*

Accent The phonology or pronunciation of a specific regional variety of a language

Agglutinating language A language in which separable morphological categories typically occur together in one word, as in Turkish → *Isolating language*, *Inflecting language*

Americanism A word, phrase or spelling that is typical of American English

Analogy The adjustment of words, grammatical forms or sounds to the major linguistic pattern

Analytic language A language that uses very few bound morphemes, its words being mostly one-syllable morphemes or compounds, as in Present-day English → *Synthetic language*

Anglo-Frisian One of the groups of West Germanic languages, including Old English and Old Frisian

Anglo-Norman The variety of English spoken by the Normans who had settled in England in medieval times → *Central French*

Anglo-Saxon An English person of the period before the Norman conquest; Old English

Anglo-Saxon heptarchy The seven Old English kingdoms Mercia, Northumbria, East Anglia, Essex, Kent, Sussex and Wessex

Aspect The verbal categories perfect and progressive

Assimilation A process by which a segment becomes more like or identical to another

Back-Mutation → *Velar Umlaut*

Borrowing The incorporation of a word in one's language from another language

Breaking A sound change in Old English, by which velarized (back) consonants (*h*, *h* + cons, *r* + cons., *l* + cons.) caused front vowels to diphthongize

Britannic → *Cymric*

Broadening A semantic change in which the meaning of a word becomes more extensive → *narrowing*

Carolingian minuscule The Norman style of handwriting, characterized by angular letter shapes → *insular Hand*

Celt A member of a race of people from western Europe who settled in ancient Britain before the Romans came

Celtic Connected with the Celts or their language

Central French The dialect spoken in Paris in medieval times, which later became standard French → *Anglo-Norman*

Centum languages Mostly Western Indo-European languages in which the Indo-European *k* either remained a *k* or shifted to *h* → *Satem languages*

Chancery hand The handwriting used by the Norman scribes at the English court, which is responsible for certain Present-day English spellings → *Carolingian minuscule, insular hand*

Chaucerisms Words used by Chaucer that had become obsolete, but were reintroduced into Early Modern English by poets

Cognates Words of different languages which are to some degree related in meaning and pronunciation because they have a common ancestor

Comparative linguistics The branch of linguistics that deals with language change by comparing related languages

Cymric (also called *Britannic*) A group of Celtic languages; its modern representatives are Welsh and Breton → *Goidelic*

Danelaw The northern part of England, which was governed by the Danes and was subject to Danish law in Late Old English times

Daughter language A descendant of an earlier form of a language → *Parent language*

Diacritics Symbols combined with segment symbols to specify various phonetic properties; extra marks added to a written character

Dialect A language variety used by a particular group of speakers → *Regional dialect*

Diphthongization A change of a vowel sound into a combination of two vowel sounds → *Monophthongization*

Dissociation The fact that many Latinate borrowings are not connected to other semantically related words in the English language

Doublets Double borrowings that have been borrowed at different periods which are not felt to be identical in form and content

Etymology The history of words; the study of the history of words

False friend A word in a foreign language that looks similar to a word in one's own language, but has a different meaning

Family tree of languages A diagram that shows the relationship between related languages over a long period of time

First Sound Shift → *Grimm's Law*

Folk Etymology Gradual change in the form of a word through the influence of a more familiar word with which it becomes associated

Front Mutation → *I-Umlaut*

Futhorc The runic alphabet, from the names of its first six letters

Gaelic → *Goidelic*

General American The American English standard, associated with the accent heard in the area of the so-called Sunbelt (from Virginia to southern California)

Germanic A branch of Indo-European to which English belongs

Gloss A note or comment added to a piece of writing to explain a difficult word or phrase

Glossary A list of technical or special words, especially those in a particular text, explaining their meanings

Goidelic (also called *Gaelic*) A group of Celtic languages from which Irish Gaelic and Scottish Gaelic have survived until today → *Cymric*

Gradation (also called *Ablaut*) A set of Indo-European vowel alternations, as in the infinitive, preterite singular, preterite plural and past participle of strong verbs

Great Vowel Shift One of *the* major (if not the major) sound shifts of English as a result of which long vowels were either raised or diphthongized (15th-17th century)

Grimm's Law (after Jakob Grimm, also called *First Sound Shift*) A systematic sound shift that is characteristic of *Germanic*, in which aspirated voiced stops became voiced fricatives and then voiced stops; voiceless stops became voiceless fricatives, and voiced stops became voiceless stops → *Verner's Law*

Hard words Mainly Latinate borrowings used in formal written Early Modern English which were difficult to understand and remember

Historical linguistics The branch of linguistics that deals with how languages change, what kinds of changes occur, and why

Indo-European language (also called *Proto-Indo-European* and *Indo-Germanic*) The ancestor of most European and some Asian languages (Sanskrit, Hindi, Persian)

Indo-Germanic → *Indo-European*

Infallibility of sound laws One of the main hypotheses of the *Neogrammarians* who claimed that sound change is regular and without exceptions

Inflecting language A language in which the morphological categories are typically fused together in a word and cannot be separated neatly from one another, as in Latin → *Agglutinating language, Isolating language*

Inkhorn terms Latin loanwords that were used in early Modern English and were considered to be prestigious; their use was often ridiculed by their opponents → *Chaucerisms*

Interlinear glosses Comments or words written between the lines in a text, e.g. word for word translations of Latin texts in Old English times

Insular hand The style of writing generally used in Old English, characterized by curved forms; an Irish version of the Roman alphabet → *Carolingian minuscule*

Irregular verbs Present-day English verbs that show a regular tense pattern → *Regular verbs*

Isolating language A language in which each word typically consists of just one morpheme, as in Vietnamese → *Agglutinating Language, Inflecting Language*

I-Mutation → *I-Umlaut*

I-Umlaut (also called *I-Mutation* or *Front Mutation*) A sound shift in Old English, as a result of which an [ɪ] or [j] caused vowels in the preceding syllable to front or to raise

Junggrammatiker → *Neogrammarians*

Language family A group of related languages

Language purists Prescriptivists who attempt to establish a particular language usage as the only correct one

Latin alphabet The letter-shapes which were used by the Romans, and which are now common in many alphabetic writing systems of the world → *Runic alphabet*

Lingua Franca A shared language of communication used by people whose native languages are different

Loan word → *Borrowing*

Malapropism The unintentional misuse of a word by confusion with one of similar sound (after Mrs. Malaprop in Sheridan's play, *The Rivals* 1775)

Meaning shift A semantic change in which the meaning of a word changes in time

Minim-problem The difficulty of distinguishing letters with upstrokes (⟨m, n, u, v, i, u⟩); solved by using the letter ⟨y⟩ for ⟨i⟩, ⟨o⟩ for ⟨u⟩, ⟨ou⟩ for ⟨ū⟩ and ⟨v⟩ for ⟨u⟩ in front of ⟨n⟩; this problem arose through the introduction of the → *Carolingian minuscule* by the Norman scribes

Monophthongization A change of a combination of two vowel sounds into a simple vowel → *Diphthongization*

Mutation → *Velar Umlaut, I-Umlaut*

Narrowing A semantic change in which the meaning of a word becomes less extensive → *broadening*

Neogrammarians A group of scholars (Karl Brugmann, August Leskien, Berthold Delbrück, Hermann Osthoff, Hermann Paul) who wished to make linguistics an exact science, in accordance with the natural sciences (19th century)

Norman French A dialect of French spoken by the Normans when they came to England

Open Syllable Lengthening A sound change in Early Middle English, as a result of which short stressed vowels were lengthened and sometimes also lowered in open syllables

Palatal diphthongization A sound change in Old English, as a result of which palatal consonants caused front vowels to diphthongize

Parent language An earlier form of a language → *Daughter language*

Phonetic spelling Adjustment of spelling to pronunciation → *Spelling pronunciation*

Polysemy A word is said to be polysemous if it has several closely related but slightly different meanings

Popular etymology → *Folk etymology*

Preterite-present verb A verb that has a strong past tense with a present meaning

Proto-Germanic → *Germanic*

Proto-Indo-European → *Indo-European*

Protolanguage An extinct and unrecorded language reconstructed by comparison of its recorded or living descendants

Received Pronunciation (RP) The standard form of British pronunciation, based on educated speech in southern England

Reconstruction The process of establishing the forms of words in a parent language by means of comparing the daughter languages → *Parent language, Daughter language*

Regional dialect The dialect spoken by people in a particular area of the language community

Regular verbs Present-day English verbs that show a regular tense pattern → *Irregular verbs*

Runic alphabet The letter-shapes that people in northern Europe used in ancient times and carved on wood or stone → *Latin alphabet*

Sanskrit A language of ancient India which belongs to the Indo-European languages

Satem languages Mostly Eastern Indo-European languages in which the Indo-European *k* shifted to a sibilant ([s], [ʃ]) → *Centum languages*

Secondary motivation → *Folk etymology*

Spelling pronunciation
   Adjustment of pronunciation to spelling → *Phonetic spelling*

Stammbaumtheorie A theory about the relatedness of languages, developed by August Schleicher in the 19th century which postulates that languages form family trees

Standard English A prestigious and codified variety of written English which emerged during the 15th century and is based on the East Midland dialect of Middle English, especially the dialect of London

Strong adjectives Adjectives that were declined strong in Old English when they were not preceded by a demonstrative or possessive → *Weak adjectives*

Strong verbs Verbs that indicate change of tense by a modification of their root vowel → *Weak verbs*

Substrate (substratum) A less socially prestigious language or linguistic variety that has influenced the structure or use of a more dominant language or variety within a community. This was particularly evidenced when in the course of colonization a language such as English or French was imposed on other people → *Superstratum*

Sunbelt The southern and south-western parts of the US

Superstratum A more socially prestigious language or linguistic variety which has influenced the structure or use of a less prestigious language or variety. It is especially the result of social, economical and political dominance of the speakers of one language over another culture.

Synonymy Words or expressions are said to be synonymous if they have the same, or nearly the same, meaning

Synthetic language A language that uses large numbers of bound morphemes, for instance inflectional suffixes, as in Old English → *Analytic language*

Velar Umlaut (also called *Back-Mutation*)
   An Old English sound change, as a result of which back vowels caused preceding front vowels to diphthongize

Verner's Law It states that noninitial voiceless fricatives in Proto-Germanic became voiced fricatives if the previous syllable had been unstressed in Proto-Indo-European

Weak adjectives Adjectives that were declined weak in Old English, which was the case when the adjectives followed a demonstrative or a possessive adjective → *Strong adjectives*

Weak verbs Verbs that indicate change of tense by the addition of a dental suffix → *Strong verbs*

BIBLIOGRAPHY

Aitchison, Jean [3]2001 [1981]. *Language Change: Process or Decay*? Cambridge: Cambridge University Press.

Algeo, John [4]1993 [1966]. *Problems in 'The Origins and the Development of the English Language'*. Fort Worth: Harcourt Brace Jovanovich.

Barber, Charles 1993. *The English Language. A Historical Introduction*. Cambridge: Cambridge University Press.

Baugh, Albert C. and Thomas Cable [4]1993 [1951]. *A History of the English Language*. London: Routledge.

Beowulf. Translated by Seamus Heaney 1999. London: Faber & Faber.

Beowulf and the Fight at Finnsburg. Edited by Fr. Klaeber [3]1950 [1922]. Lexington, Mass.: D.C. Heath Company.

Biber, Douglas (ed.) 1999. *Longman Grammar of Spoken and Written English*. Harlow: Longman.

The Book of Margery Kempe. Edited by Sanford Brown Meech 1940. London: Oxford University Press.

Cable, Thomas [2]1993. *A Companion to Baugh and Cable's History of the English Language*. Englewood Cliffs: Prentice Hall.

Campbell, Alistair 1959. *Old English Grammar*. London: Oxford University Press.

Cawdrey, Robert 1604. *A Table Alphabeticall of Hard Words*. London: Printed by I. R. for Edmund Weaver.

Crystal, David 1988. *The English Language. A guided tour of the language by the presenter of BBC Radio 4's English now*. London: Penguin.

Crystal, David 1995. *The Cambridge Encyclopedia of the English Language*. Cambridge: Cambridge University Press.

Crystal, David 1997. *English as a Global Language*. Cambridge: Cambridge University Press.

Faiß, Klaus 1989. *Englische Sprachgeschichte*. Tübingen: Francke.

Fischer, Roswitha 1998. *Lexical Change in Present-day English. A corpus-based study of the motivation, institutionalization, and productivity of creative neologisms*. Tübingen: Gunter Narr.

Freeborn, Dennis [2]1998 [1992]. *From Old English to Standard English. A course book in language variation across time*. Basingstoke: Macmillan.

Gimson A.C. and Alan Cruttenden [5]1994 [1962]. *Gimson's Pronunciation of English*. London: Edward Arnold.

Görlach, Manfred 1978. *Introduction to Early Modern English*. Cambridge: Cambridge University Press.

Graddol, David 1997. *The Future of English? A guide to forecasting the popularity of the English languae in the 21st century*. London: British Council.

Grimm, Jacob 1819/1837. *Deutsche Grammatik*, 4 vols. Göttingen.

The Holy Bible, Conteyning the Old Testament, and the New: Newly Translated out of the Originall tongues: & with the former Translations diligently compared and reuised, by his Maiesties speciall Commandment. Appointed to be read in Churches. Edited by W. A. Wright 1909. Cambridge.

Kachru, Braj B. 1985. "Standards, Codification and Sociolinguistic Realism: The English Language in the Outer Circle." In Randolph Quirk and H. G. Widdowson (eds.), *English in the World*. Cambridge: Cambridge University Press. 11-30.

Kortmann, Bernd 2001. "In the Year 2525... Reflections on the Future Shape of English." In *Anglistik. Mitteilungen des Deutschen Anglistenverbandes*, edited by Rüdiger Ahrens, 12.1.: 97-114.

Lass, Roger 1987. *The Shape of English*. London: J.M. Dent & Sons.

Lass, Roger 1994. *Old English. A Historical Linguistic Companion* Cambridge: Cambridge University Press.

Leisi, Ernst and Christian Mair [8]1999 [1955]. *Das heutige Englisch: Wesenszüge und Probleme*. Heidelberg: Winter.

Leith, Dick 1983. *A Social History of English*. London: Routledge & Kegan Paul.

Mair, Christian and Marianne Hundt 1995. „Why Is the Progressive Becoming More Frequent in English? A Corpus-Based Investigation of Language Change in Progress." *Zeitschrift für Anglistik und Amerikanistik* 2. 111-122.

Marckwardt, Albert H. and Joey L. Dillard [2]1980 [1958]. *American English*. New York: Oxford University Press.

McMahon, April M. S. 1994. *Understanding Language Change*. Cambridge: Cambridge University Press.

Mitchell, Bruce 1995. *An Invitation to Old English and Anglo-Saxon England*. Oxford: Blackwell.

Mitchell, Bruce and Fred C. Robinson [5]1992 [1964]. *A Guide to Old English*. Oxford: Blackwell.

Moessner, Lilo and Ursula Schaefer [2]1987 [1974]. *Proseminar Mittelenglisch*. Tübingen: Francke.

Mossé, Fernand. [3]1986 [1973]. *Mittelenglische Kurzgrammatik*. München: Max Hueber.

The New English Bible. The Old Testament. 1970. Oxford and Cambridge University Press.

Obst, Wolfgang and Florian Schleburg 1999. *Die Sprache Chaucers. Ein Lehrbuch des Mittelenglischen auf der Grundlage von Troilus and Criseyde*. Heidelberg: Winter.

The Oxford Advanced Learner's Dictionary of Current English. Edited by A. S. Hornby and and Sally Wehmeier [6]2000 [1948]. Oxford: Oxford University Press.

The Oxford Guide to English Usage [2]1993 [1983]. Compiled by E. S. C. Weiner und Andrew Delahunty. London: Oxford University Press.

Pennycook, Alastair 1998. *English and the Discourses of Colonialism*. London: Routledge.

Phillipson, Robert 1992. *Linguistic Imperialism*. Oxford: Oxford University Press.

Piers Plowman by William Langland. Edited by Derek Pearsall 1978. London: Edward Arnold.

The Riverside Shakespeare. Edited by G. Blakemore Evans 1974. Boston: Houghton Mifflin.

Sauer, Walter [2]1990 [1979]. *A Drillbook of English Phonetics*. Heidelberg, Carl Winter Universitätsverlag.

Strang, Barbara 1970. *A History of English*. London: Methuen.

Trudgill, Peter and Jean Hannah [3]1994 [1982]. *International English. A guide to varieties of standard English*. London: Arnold.

Wells, John C. 1982. *Accents of English 1: An Introduction*. Cambridge: Cambridge University Press.

The Works of Geoffrey Chaucer. Edited by F. N. Robinson [2]1976. London: Oxford University Press.

Yule, George [2]1996 [1985]. *The Study of Language*. Cambridge: Cambridge University Press.